SATURDAY NIGHT
IN *Baoding*

SATURDAY NIGHT
IN *Baoding*

A CHINA MEMOIR

Richard Terrill

The University of Arkansas Press

Fayetteville   London   1990

Designer: Chang-hee H. Russell
Typeface: Linotron 202 Cartier
Typesetter: G&S Typesetters, Inc.
Printer: Edwards Brothers, Inc.
Binder: Edwards Brothers, Inc.

The paper used in this publication meets the minimum requirements of the
American National Standard for Permanence of Paper for Printed Library
Materials z39.48-1984. ∞

Library of Congress Cataloging-in-Publication Data

Terrill, Richard, 1953–
      Saturday night in Baoding : a china memoir / Richard Terrill.
          p.   cm.
      ISBN 1-55728-132-7 (alk. paper). — ISBN 1-55728-133-5 (pbk. : alk. paper)
      1. China—Description and travel—1976–   2. Terrill, Richard,
      1953–   —Journeys—China.   I. Title.
      DS712.T38   1990
      915.104′58—dc20   89-20276
                                                                    CIP

To protect individuals' identities, some names have been changed in this
narrative, some composite characters created, and some events altered slightly.

Not quite three years after I left China, thousands of college students were murdered in Beijing on orders from the Chinese Communist Party.
This book is dedicated to their memory.

CONTENTS

ACKNOWLEDGMENTS

Excerpts from this book, sometimes in a different form, have appeared in *New Letters*, *Another Chicago Magazine*, and *Hawaii Pacific Review*.

For their generous help I would like to thank Bruce Taylor, Bill Carpenter, John Hildebrand, Cui Shuqin, Chen Yubao, Susan Whitlock, and the Chinese-American Educational Exchange.

The Wisconsin Arts Board, with funding from the National Endowment for the Arts, provided me with a grant which lent support and encouragement.

I, on my side, require of every writer, first or last, a simple and sincere account of his own life, and not merely what he has heard of other men's lives; some such account as he would send to his kindred from a distant land, for if he has lived sincerely, it must have been in a distant land to me.

Henry David Thoreau
Walden

SATURDAY NIGHT
IN *Baoding*

DANCING

Last night a German couple from the education department taught a roomful of Chinese students to dance. *One-two, cha cha cha.* No, a German couple was teaching a roomful of Chinese students some new steps. They already knew how to dance. Only I didn't know how to dance; I'm an American.

Ballroom dancing is the rage among young people in northern China, in Baoding, where I teach. Waltz, tango, four-step, jitterbug. Disco is still not officially sanctioned. "We're too close to Beijing," some people will tell you. "It breaks up the family," I heard one young man say.

"Next ve vill learn the jive," said Gunther, the German Sinologist. "You move left, you move right." The Chinese were getting it; I felt like I wasn't. Why did I misspend my youth on rock-and-roll? On books and studies? "Keep at it," said Greta, his wife. "You're not hopeless."

Only two short years ago, my students tell me, they danced behind locked doors in their dorm rooms, in their classrooms at night, chairs pushed aside. If someone outside the door asked, "What are you doing?" they said, "We are listening to music," and the person went away, almost as if the person knew that some midlevel cadre in the capital, no doubt with the blessing of

Deng Xiaoping himself, would decide that dancing was not bourgeois after all, and with that, overnight, as if someone had thrown a switch on millions of national Christmas trees, China would begin to dance.

Almost as if he knew that on the coattails of the four modernizations—agriculture, science and technology, industry, the military—rode all the others: music, dancing, make-up, stylish clothes, and fast food. People tell me that China is changing. I know only that these coattails are long and that some of this decadence will be clinging to them. Perhaps we haven't seen the end of that coat, perhaps there are more changes to come. The long-suffering Chinese hope there are.

So far, there's dance. It's good exercise, the Party says, and so the young Chinese dance holding each other at arm's length, or nearly so. There's no danger of titillation, only a workout. I'm in awe at the lack of sexuality. Though my junior students, the boys, have confessed this is their one chance each week to meet the girls, you wouldn't know it. I think we Americans must sprinkle sexuality on our cereal. Have sexuality in our formula as infants. Here, everyone seems intent on the business of movement, of getting it right. Girls dance with boys, girls dance with girls. Indeed boys dance with boys, and even soldiers with soldiers. There's little overt or covert in this dance, sexual or otherwise. The steps are well planned, rehearsed, performed. Everyone's good, or looks as if he wants to be. Surely this is the grace people in America have been talking about for years, this business of the repetition of a beautiful act so that it becomes thoughtless and thus provokes the thought of the observer. The tango, for instance, is a beautiful dance, my students tell me. The dancers look very beautiful.

It's Saturday night. We're in the dining hall, tables pushed aside à la sock hop. The tables wear their ever-present coat of grease, unwiped after weeks of meals, so unfit are they even to lean against; so it's dance or drop of museum feet, of wallflower disease. There's still a circle of bystanders around the already crowded dance floor, but the circle will grow thinner, the floor more populous as the night wears on inevitably toward eleven P.M. There's a dim yellow that hangs about the room in spite of the one bright light in the corner over which a sheet of colored plastic turns—again à la seventh grade—so that the yellow of the room is colored slightly by red, then blue, then more yellow. There's a series of brown stains, like marks of old water from a leaky roof or pipes, visible on most every wall despite the dim light. The music oozes out of a loud three-piece band in one corner into the warehouse-sized room. The sound is generically high and thin like ten living room organs, like a chorus of comb and tissue paper. The band sounds like its members were locked in a room for a week and told to learn to like each other. The keyboard player holds one chord through "Auld Lang Syne." There's a Strauss waltz, some beats dropped into Moon River. A few Chinese pop tunes I've learned to recognize. The rest, pure notes.

Two weeks in China, and I have to learn to dance. My girl students have asked me, and now the boys are beginning to. I'm nearly out of excuses: No, young people don't dance this way in America. Yes, maybe disco. But also rock-and-roll. "Rock-and-roll, you know?" I ask. They nod, but they don't.

I wish that I could dance. Dance well and be the center of attention, like I am when I walk down the dusty streets here—blond and bearded—like I came here to be. A pretty student will teach me, surely . . . maybe Guo Xiaoming, my Chinese language tutor, already acutely aware of what I'm not capable of.

"First put your legs here, among my legs."

"All of them?"

"No, among my legs."

I do it wrong, but she persists. She holds my left hand up high like in a square dance when others are to pass underneath. I feel like some kind of teetering statue, a precarious bird, feeling everyone is watching him. Everyone is.

"Now forward, together. Back. Together. Yes, that's right."

So reassuring! So easy! To come here, a world away, to learn to dance as my father did when he met my mother! This will help me get past the literal: the donkey carts, the coal smoke, the crowds, the factories, the bicycles, the mud streets of Baoding. The secret to understanding China is . . . ballroom dancing. This is no longer Western dance, not my culture; it is hers, it is theirs, the communal innocence that becomes warm in time like the yellow light in the big room of the world. There's no beer at this dance. This is not America. No squealing tires, no puking in the parking lot. No parking lot. No coat check. No orchestra. No moonlit garden walk. Tonight, no moon—perhaps, hidden by clouds, it's been broken up in pieces, divided equally among the peasants. There's no fountain, no promenade. There's hardly even music as we know it, except for the whistle of a distant steam engine I think no one hears but me. There's only the dance. Civilized and predictable. So totally and obviously re-creative. A wholesomeness where wholesome is not yet a dirty word. The dirt here is on the walls, not in the mind. It's on the tables where we eat, in the dust in the streets, and it's real and is the kind that washes off, once a week. Dancing here is not a craze after all. It's an allowance that must be spent. Some students, I'm told, cross town to the art college for Friday's dance, Saturday at our university not being enough for them. Dancing here is pleasure in a life of little pleasure, a life where pleasure was, and still is, viewed with suspicion. When the lights go up at the end of the evening, they don't go up far—electricity is precious. There's no lingering, but instead people crowd for the door because outside is night and responsibility six days a week—to self, to family, ostensibly to the revolution. I'm the last to leave.

I have a mild dose of culture shock. From the year I lived in South Korea, I recognize the symptoms: waking up in the morning tired, feeling afternoons like I want to pull some great blanket over my head, curl up in fetal position, and think about how warm the color gray is when the curtains are drawn against that place that is inescapable, that *out there*. My culture shock has been brought on by one of those singularly Chinese phenomena, that of the "disappearing friend." It's something I'd heard and read has happened to others.

My story concerns Guo Xiaoming. My Chinese language tutor and my dance instructor of Saturday night, she is bright and lively, harmless and innocent. She has a slight stutter when she speaks—

even in Chinese, I've noticed—which I attribute to a kind of excess energy in pursuing life, mixed with an honest insecurity so that she has too many directions to go all at once, too many things she could possibly say in a given situation. There is a kind of stumbling concern to her intelligence, so that when she taught me to dance, for instance, she was able to reassure even as she groped for words to communicate with me: "Put your foot here. Yes, that's right. Put your legs among my legs." "One two, now back, one two, now turn, yes you have it," she'd say again and again, never saying I had it when in fact I didn't, but never letting me think there was a chance I couldn't learn, when in fact there was always a chance I wouldn't.

Her intelligence, her quickness had another dimension not lost on the foreigner—an ability to communicate, to quickly bridge the gap of culture. It took her so little time, for example, to get by the elementary level of questioning to which any group of people will subject a foreigner: Where are you from? How long will you stay in China? Is this your first time to China? At what university do you teach in America? And so on. I don't even remember her asking these questions. I think she just listened as others in the group asked them. That is, she listened *to* the answers rather than listen *for an* answer as one does who is learning a language and wants to check if he's making contact in that other language. She, preferring to hear the answers, would then ask me more personal, insightful questions based on what she heard. So it would be not "How long will you stay in China?" but "Why did you want to come here?" Not "Where are you from?" but "It must be very different from Baoding." Not "Why aren't you dancing?" but "It's very easy; let me teach you."

More than the others she made us feel (for there were two of us Americans in Baoding, a city of three hundred thousand), rightly or not, that she wanted to know us rather than just practice her English. I noticed an aura about her: childlike excitement, yet her concern so apparent in her serious look. When she smiled, as she often did, it was a smile not of the mouth or just the mouth and eyes, but a smile of the face, as if in the wholeness of that gesture lay her openness to what would happen in the next moment and the next. There was a touch of self-consciousness always in her serious expression, in the intense dark eyes that so desperately darted about to search for a word or idea. So intense was this occupation with what was being said or understood by her that when she smiled so quickly it had the effect on the other of diving into water, or perhaps diving into water only to land instead in someone's arms. I think in her face was the look—so rare in China, I was to find—that said she would relinquish control, be willing to follow someone's lead to see if there was something she could learn or gain from it.

There was something boyish about her looks that made her, strangely, more feminine. It was in the way she walked—hands in pockets, just-too-large steps, an even pace, slightly bouncing. Something about her walk made me think she should be on her way to a sandlot baseball game. And there was her special innocence. When I asked why her roommates were not at the dance, she said somewhat coyly they were secretly meeting their boyfriends, leaving clearly the implication that she hadn't one.

I think there was also in her an innocence about people's motives, about the small things in the world which people will take on for their personal gain, or worse, to bring about a loss to the innocent one. But maybe I'm wanting to see too much in her.

One day in class—this was after two more Saturday nights, two more dances—I knew something had happened. The bright face of Guo Xiaoming was swollen over ever so slightly from a new kind of seriousness, not one of concern but of forced distance, of correction. Her eyes were darker, buried in her book or aimed at the gray floor. She did not speak or look at me, and when I called on her to answer a question about a Hemingway story, she could look away from me without taking her eyes from mine, so much hurt and distance were there in her eyes.

"Someone talked to her," the Germans explained to me. They were old China hands, in Baoding for a visit—Gunther fluent in Chinese, Greta the confidante of many young Chinese women. "Or worse, people are talking about her. 'She's spending too much time with the foreigner,' they're saying. 'Psst, psst, psst,' you know?

"Someone gets jealous and goes to the Party leader in the Department: 'She was seen leaving the foreigner's apartment alone,' or some such thing."

That much was true: she'd come by twice to conduct my Chinese lessons—with official permission.

"'On Saturday night they dance.'" the Germans continued. "'They smile. He dances with others, but not as much. This is wrong thinking.'"

Western influence? Decadence? I can only guess what the exact nature of the sin is. But a rumor is started. Intentionally. The word is passed, first by a Party member in the class, maybe on to Party members in other classes and on to other students. Very soon everyone—not evilly but just out of boredom, as people will—takes up the talk. Soon something meant innocently is no longer innocent.

I knew I was testing the system somewhat, but I didn't think the result would be something so sudden and unsubtle. I didn't think there was any permanent damage done to her, to her chance to be successful here, and happy, as she is surely meant to be. I think the loss is mine; I lost a friend. My first here. Someone that I thought in a short time I could say something more important to than "I am from Chicago." My German friends had called her my shadow; I didn't know it would be so apparent to others—I should have known, since in nothing I do here can I be inconspicuous. So at the risk of being romantic over what really is a small matter, I can say that if my shadow is gone then the light too must be gone, or lessened so that I cannot see objectively, see clearly or well.

Some months later, on a Saturday night, the weekly dancing party is canceled. I decide to go to a movie at the PLA (People's Liberation Army) hospital with three senior girl students. One of them is Guo Xiaoming. Through these months I've taught her American literature, and she's been my Chinese tutor on Thursday nights. But she's always conducted the lessons accompanied by her friend from the sophomore class, never alone.

This night she is at her best, giggling and bright. At my suggestion, since we are late for the movie, we engage in a walking race to the hospital—heel and toe, heel and toe. For some reason, her laughter this night makes me care not at all that others walking to the movie stare at our silliness. I almost feel like inviting their attention, then ignoring it to show how good I feel when she feels free to act and be herself. We soon leave our friends behind as we wiggle, heel and toe, down the dirt street past other moviegoers and the creaking donkey carts of a few peasants going home late from town. The leaves on the trees seem to rustle as we walk by, laughing, and soon I open up a big lead on her, probably making me look more ridiculous.

I stop to wait for her, then suggest the next leg of our competition be a running-backwards race. Occasionally peeking over our shoulders, swerving around the holes and rocks in the road, we are neck and neck—or, I should say, butt and butt—the rest of the way, getting to the theater a good three minutes before our friends.

The movie is somewhat of an oddity for me in the same way the dancing party proves to be most weeks. I find myself in a packed theater watching, dubbed in Chinese, a British children's film about a gypsy boy who rescues a girl from a cave—the kind of thing that's shown in the States on Sunday afternoon after a football game—and then what I suspect is a U.S. made-for-TV version of *The Man in the Iron Mask* with Richard Chamberlain. Also, of course, dubbed, as all foreign movies here are.

My own fallen standards of entertainment aside, the night is delightful, and I remind Miss Guo of her promise to come by the next Saturday afternoon to teach me to tango, the one dance step I haven't yet been able to learn. Before I go to bed that night I think for a long while about Guo Xiaoming.

That next weekend the appointed hour of her coming passes and there is no knock at my door. Later she tells me the Saturday afternoon political meeting lasted later than usual. Also that Miss Wei Fengyun, her dancing partner, has a very bad cold and couldn't come to my room with her. But I think she is still frightened from the incident in the fall. I think she won't come alone to any man's apartment, least of all an unmarried foreigner.

A CHICAGOAN
IN CHINA

◪ The political problems that led to the disappearing friend notwithstanding, I find that most Chinese are so nice that after three weeks of language lessons with Guo Xiaoming and with my other tutors I think I understand Chinese already. Actually I can pick out only a few common phrases—as if my life were a movie with scratchy subtitles. Today, for instance, the only one in a room, I had to answer a ringing phone, and before I could recite my line—literally, "I no can speak Chinese"—the other party was off and talking and he obviously hadn't been studying the same Chinese lesson book that I had. When I finally did tell him I couldn't understand, he sounded so nice about it that I just kept nodding *dui, dui, dui, dui, dui*—yes, yes, yes, yes, yes—for several minutes. I was only brought back to cruel reality when he hung up suddenly—though it probably wasn't sudden to him because he knew what he was talking about.

Learning to speak Chinese is a bit like teaching a parakeet to sing, only you're the parakeet. One slip, one wrong tone and you've chirped a word you didn't mean to. So that SHUUU with a flat tone—book—can become SHU*uuu* with a falling tone—tree. To memorize that, you have to think that trees fall down, while books usually don't. If you mess it up, the penalty is severe: you can't, after all, read trees.

Except perhaps in China. Here trees are easier for the non-speaking foreigner to understand, their language greener in this the land of dust. More foreigners, when they think of China, should think of dust. Most think of ancient dynasties, or Mao Zedong, or chopsticks. That's misinformed. The emperors are long gone. Mao Zedong is rolling over in his mausoleum at the sight of free markets in every city and town, the so-called "responsibility system." The government even tried to do away with chopsticks and common plates for reasons of sanitation, although it proved easier to get rid of the emperors and the cult of Maoism than it did the chopsticks.

Some Westerners think too, thinking of China, of the Great Wall. That's misguided. Think of the Great Cloud. Dust. Brown dust, or reddish in the Southwest, I'm told. So when the dust blows through the trees, the leaves whisper. The trees are here in China to hold up the sky, one thinks; the air is that tangible. Walking, you have to step around it. You might hurt yourself running into it.

SHUUU—book.

SHU*uuu*— tree.

Learning Chinese, there are so many ways to fail. I'm trying to say *bathroom* and, misplacing tones, have made some comment, Guo Xiaoming tells me, about someone's feet. But she is bright and charming and laughs easily, making fun out of something so difficult—as much fun as it can be to reshape the inside of your mouth without kissing anyone. For instance: *Zhi-jia-ge*. All first tones, all even tones. That's easy. I live in *Zhi-jia-ge*. All over China they seem to know about it, those who speak English, those I can talk to. "*Zhijiage* is known as the windy city!" they tell me.

"*Dui, dui, dui, dui, dui,*" I say.

But something is wrong: *Bu zhu zai Zhi jia ge,*" not Chicago. Baoding. Now I live in Baoding. *Xianzai wo zhu zai Baoding.*

And what is there to see, to say about Baoding? Donkey chip capital of eastern China? Second City of Hebei Province? (We were once the provincial capital and main city, but now our New York is down the road in Shijiazhuang.)

My sophomore students wrote assignment number one, "What a Foreigner Should Know about Baoding City." "Keep in your mind," writes one, "that Baoding is *famous* for pickled vegetables. But I'm afraid to you they will not be delicious."

He was wrong; to me they are delicious, but I wonder at my students' overuse of the word "famous." In Chinese, they say *you ming*, which they could translate as "well known," but they don't. Thus the dining hall on campus, which the students freely admit serves terrible food, might be "famous" for its steamed bread. Miss Chen might be "famous" on campus for badminton. The Chinese pronounce the English word as "fame-erce," which adds to the charm.

"And keep in your mind that Baoding is also famous for Baoding Iron Balls," another student writes, for manufactured here are pairs of shiny, larger-than-golf-ball-sized metal spheres that as children we would have called "steelies" in our marble games. It seems you hold both in one hand and maneuver them in a circular pattern—like Humphrey Bogart in *The Caine Mutiny*. They're supposed to develop coordination and dexterity, and they're particularly popular among old people. Unlike our steelies, they have little bells inside that ring as the balls are turned. I found out later that some enterprising young businessman had tried to export Baoding Iron Balls to the States as the latest yuppie toy. I hear he was left with a basement full of them, like so many miniature lawn ornaments.

The students' paragraphs didn't answer the needs of my curiosity. What is there to see, to do in Baoding? I would have to find out for myself: nothing. And everything.

There is, first, outside the gate of my university, the mark of the New China. That is, of the new New China, the one with free markets, Deng Xiaoping's "Responsibility System." They squat there a good part of the day, troops of peasants beside their fruits and vegetables, earning, I'm told, much more than they can selling solely to the State. Some of them in fact will try to charge me for a few apples twice as much as the Chinese pay. Mao Zedong, who believed there was no human nature, but only class nature, might have called this exploitation. But I don't mind terribly. I think, haggling with the merchants, that buying and selling things is as human as breathing, maybe more so in Baoding's coalish air. Trying to get a decent price is also human nature, and so I cross the road for a better deal from another vendor—dodging army trucks, unmarked open manholes, and the much celebrated Chinese sea of bicycles (that's understatement—the bicycles are not so much water as the walker is an island, maybe the island of Atlantis).

In Chicago, every Saturday, I'd take the Clark Street bus down to Lincoln Park—ninety cents at that time—then walk a beat west on Fullerton and up Lincoln Avenue, stopping always at my allergist's and a couple of favorite bookstores, maybe a bar. I liked it. And then I'd walk home to my Wrigleyville apartment, trying hard to see what was new or different, seasonal or changing. Sometimes it was a new Thai restaurant, or a crew refurbishing an old brownstone. Sometimes I saw a friend or heard someone speaking a language I couldn't understand. I usually saw a lot, was seldom disappointed.

In China, I take Bus number four from the university gate downtown—it costs *yi mao*, 3.3 cents American—and in this newest of possible worlds I try to find not something new, but something familiar, the sights I remember seeing the last trip downtown and the one before. There's first the line of outdoor barber chairs across from the bus stop. Some of the barbers are busy while some sit on their haunches—never in the chair, which is reserved for customers—and read the *People's Daily*. There's one gray-maned, rather distinguished looking cutter who eyes my blond hair eagerly each time I pass, and I'm pleased, not because I'd ever go to him for a haircut—drawing a crowd there on the street that would likely stop traffic—but because I can depend on him to be there and to smile and say *ni hao*, hello, even if his is the smile of someone who wants something from me.

Not yet two months in-country, I'm looking for the familiar to prove to myself I belong here. The bus route, for instance: when the bus turns that first corner and then the second, just as I knew it would, I feel a sense of satisfaction almost as if I'd willed it to make those turns, or as if I were driving. When the bus stalls out at a stoplight, I'm not surprised anymore. When the bus fills up at the stop in front of a small open marketplace, I'm not surprised anymore either. When the bus conductor takes my money, and gives me the right ticket, understanding when I say in Chinese "I'm going downtown," I'm still a little surprised, but I don't have to admit it to anyone. I settle back into my hard seat and smile to myself. In yuppie parlance, I'm a survivor. Hell, this might be Lincoln Park: the Biograph become the Worker's Cinema, now showing the latest from Germany—East or West. Instead of Demon Dogs under the el stop at De Paul, the woman roasting sweet potatoes over an oil drum on the corner not far from the elementary school. Instead of Chicago's quiet churches on shady side streets, Baoding's one church on the busy main street, rebuilt after the Cultural Revolution by a government eager to prove its tolerance. The priest there invites to Sunday mass any Chinese brave enough to admit they are Christians. Instead of the flood of private cars and impossible parking, the flood of private carts and improbable donkeys. Instead of the Century Mall, the Number One Department Store, which is my stop.

So I get off, this being after all a shopping trip. Shopping in Baoding gives new meaning to the American upper class socialite notion of going somewhere "to be seen." There is at least one thing to see in Baoding, and I'm it. Gangs of peasants, workers, children, grandmothers follow me down the street, watch my every move, my every step. And this just because I'm from another planet—a poor excuse, it seems to me. See the foreigner open a door! Watch him turn a corner. Look, he's buying gloves—maybe he'll try them on!

One story, probably apocryphal, concerns a group of foreigners in Tianjin, a larger north China city. When asked by a pack of curious Chinese where they were from, they replied, "the moon."

"Oh," said the Chinese. "And what language do you speak on the moon?"

The traveler thinks that China could double its gross national product inside of a month if the government would just give these staring people something to do. But in the meantime, how to deal with them? Well, you can get angry; that usually gets rid of them but at a terrible price to your self-esteem. Maybe wear a mask. Or one guidebook suggests announcing you're Russian, which dampens enthusiasm hereabouts. Some advocate staring back. I've tried this, and I always win the staredowns, but after a while begin to feel like a shirt-tail relative of Bela Lugosi.

Then there's the reasoning that says if they've seen you once they won't stare so long and hard a second time. So if you can pass on the street two or three thousand Chinese a day, and if there are one billion in China, in less than one thousand years living here you ought to be able to go unnoticed pretty much anywhere you want.

Short of venturing out only at night and wearing a homicidally mean look, holding my hand in my breast pocket and making any Third Worlder recall that, of course, all Americans carry guns, I've found nothing else that completely solves the problem. I have developed several simple rules to make the problem easier to live with, rather like taking aspirin for a cold, or maybe like taking aspirin for a gunshot wound to the head.

Rule Number One: Don't go out on Sunday. On weekdays a lot of people have nothing better to do than stare at a foreigner; on Sundays no one has anything better to do than stare at a foreigner.

Rule Number Two: Walk on the right side of the street, going *with* the bicycle traffic, not on the left side, *facing* the bicycle traffic. Walking on the left makes me feel like I'm running up the down escalator. Everyone can see me, face to face, for blocks. On the right, they can look at the back of my head as long as they want and I don't know about it. If they try to crane their necks for a look at the front of me as they pass, they risk a fender bender with one or more of the thousand-odd bikes in front of them.

Rule Number Three: Keep moving. Nothing is so expensive in Boading that it's worth the trouble of trying on or out before purchase. As for stopping for photographs, I tell myself that someday those shots of crowded narrow streets will look a lot alike.

Besides the rules I have two reminders for myself. One is to wear the big bright badge—red of course—that announces in Chinese, "Hebei University." I hear people mouth the words as I pass. Knowing why I'm here—or as the Chinese say, "where I am," meaning what work unit I'm assigned to—seems to allay some of their curiosity about why I look so funny.

The other reminder is to smile. People are standing stock still with their mouths open at the sight of me. If I smile, they can't know why. Even in the land of comradely surveillance, the kingdom of gossip and innuendo that China is, that remains my business. It gives me an advantage somehow, evens the score, or at least makes me feel like it does.

Finally, there's little to compare between Chicago and Baoding, my past and present hometowns. There's more to see and do in Chicago, but it's pretty hard to get noticed there. In America, I'd like more people to notice me, especially women; in a country where everyone wants attention, few can get enough.

In China, I'm just different; in Baoding, a failure as a sightseer. How to see sights when you can't tell the sights from industry, can't distinguish tourism from the daily ebb and flow, the dust in the streets? How to court adventure when loneliness makes you crave what you already know? There is no one answer, only the remainder of my year here. And my students' compositions, which must be read and graded.

"Baoding is a beautiful city," one student concludes, "and I like it."

STEALING THE ROSES

■ I'm on my north balcony one early morning before breakfast, in hand a copy of a long letter that I wrote to Gwen before I came here. Gwen is a woman I knew for a time, not a long time, about six years ago. We were sort of "going together" then, though not many people knew about it. For some reason, before I left for Baoding, I got the idea of writing her a letter for the first time in almost the whole six years.

From this balcony I can watch, unseen myself, the activities of the morning in Baoding. At the foot of our building, four floors directly below my porch, stands our cook Lao Fan. A woman is selling meat from the back of a bicycle, a whole lamb I think, and she is cutting thin strips that Fan will cook for our lunch or dinner.

"Gaoyang rou," the woman shouts.

I haven't seen this sight before, and I want to take a picture, but I fear my intrusion will spoil the scene—as though the picture is there until I want to take it, then it's gone. The woman has spotted me now—how did she know to look four floors up?

. . . how must you think of me now? [I read in the letter before me.] I'm giving up all that's familiar to me (though it's true much of that made me un-

happy) and trying something else. Yes, there will be adventure, but I'm not going for that, as I did when I went to live in Korea. This time I want to be open to the real possibility that there's another way of thinking about things. Maybe less narrow and dark, like some alley flooded with light and life suddenly each morning. . . .

I notice that the knife with which she cuts the meat is sharp but dirty. The bicycle is black and gray, the same gray that rises from this landscape and settles over it again in the evening, replaced all day by the brown dust of the streets, spread by PLA trucks, a very occasional car or bus, and the always present horse carts and bicycles.

Before I arrived here I might have wished I hadn't witnessed the scene—the dirty knife, the common way which my food comes to me—but now somehow I'm glad for the food and for her efforts.

. . . you were right—nobody starts at the top. I remember how mad you were the night I complained about my lack of upward mobility (but we didn't call it that in those days)—i.e., that I was twenty-six and had a job I hated. I did finally get a college teaching job, but before that I worked as a musician again. Other people thought I had quite the life, but I wasn't impressed by the glitz, the lounge lizards, the Holiday Inns. I got sick of eating out all the time. . . .

From my porch I see the following: a dormitory—factory-like, six or seven students living behind each large twelve-paned glass window; to the left of that, a larger dormitory for unmarried faculty; across from that a classroom building; and next to that a small building, one side of which houses the boiler for the quasi-nightly, quasi-hot water for showers in our apartment building, which is occupied by senior and retired faculty and the foreigners: the two Americans, the two Japanese, and for this month only my German friends Gunther and Greta. Between these buildings runs a zig zag of concrete, wide enough for, say, two groups of workers and an intermittent stream of bikes to pass either way. When a horse or donkey cart comes by, someone on one side or the other must step aside for its slow progress.

. . . I'd like to grab hold of the experience before it becomes just one more bar story. I'm going to give the language a better shot than I did in Korea. I've started already: I'm up to lesson three in my Teach Yourself Chinese *book. I want to forget about being American and all that goes with it. Last time living in Asia I found I really was ethnocentric: I found myself thinking, "These people," as if they were inferior. Although I know there's no understanding it, this time I want to allow for culture: that they may not like me finally, or I them, and that's all right. I don't know if this makes sense to you or not. . . .*

Some of the walkers pass to my left (and of course four floors below me) carrying silver pots or brightly colored thermoses—most of them red—on their way to and from another building behind the dormitories, the one where *kai shui*, boiling drinking water, is dispensed in taps outside, as if on a farm. As in most of Asia, water in China must be boiled for drinking, and all Chinese have these thermoses everywhere, at home, at work, even on trains. I've gotten used to drinking water hot—with or without tea—as the Chinese do. Because I am a foreigner, I need only place my thermos outside the door to have it filled in the morning. But I find that I enjoy going to fill the thermos myself every morning or evening, partaking of the distinctly Eastern joy in everyone doing something at the same time.

. . . Many people can live alone naturally from birth, and the rest of us have to learn. Since I've seen you last I've had lots of experience; living in another culture again will be more practice. Again in China I'm putting on the collar and smock. The collar is being blond and the smock is having a beard and a big nose in a part of the world where foreigners are known by that: Hey, there goes "hairy," "big nose," "round eyes." I want to be more alone than I have ever tried to be, and I want to come out of it intact in all ways, especially mentally. If I do, I feel somehow that will show me that whatever it is that's wrong with me,

what's made it difficult for me to have a stable relationship, that all that will be diminished as a force in my life. . . .

It occurs to me now that the bright color of these thermoses, these very practical articles, is the only bright color visible in this scene, maybe the only bright color in Baoding (suddenly I wonder what winter will be like). Buildings are pale red brick, streets and shops brown and gray. The sun hasn't shone since I've lived here, ten days now. And the dress of the older people is what an American expects it will be—gray, brown, khaki, or mostly dull blue; formless army shirts and pants, what we in the West call Mao jackets. Only some of the younger people, the college students on what is after all a campus, wear a nice sweater or tighter fitting pants. And the children dress brightly. One is passing now, pulled by his mother in a two-wheeled cart. He's in red and green, like a flower, with a bright orange cap, brighter than a deer hunter would wear in Wisconsin, where I grew up.

. . . I'm told that my town's only recently opened to foreigners, so the staring squads will be outrageous. And there will be my pitiful attempts at speaking a tonal language, where a different pitch means a different word, not just a different feeling as in English: rising inflection, question; falling and short, the imperative; lilting and soft, love or romance. It's so easy for us in our native tongue, not having to worry about meaning, but only what we mean. . . .

No one sees me on the balcony. The movement of the people, mostly middle-aged or older, is light. Some stop to talk with one another—I can all but guess what pleasantries they exchange—but most move slowly and silently, involved in routine. Where are the young people, the college students? In their rooms, I think. Later will come the mass movement to the dining hall. All five thousand, on their way to breakfast, then class. Now, a few are out for morning exercise, but no one is playing sports (that's reserved for the end of the day). I don't know how or when they get their hot water. Maybe before I get up. I know of their domestic lives only the few hanging clothes or blankets on a line in the yard in front of their dormitories.

. . . I want to try to get more out of teaching than I did last time in Asia. I miss the classroom after my pointless job in Chicago, and I'm wondering if my cynicism hasn't finally spent itself and if I can find something there that transcends the rut of work that everyone I know is in (except artists). Mostly, though, I want to be more patient than I am here. I'd like to stop keeping lists, think there is another way to look at things and think like some spent hippy that in Eastern thought lies a key to contentment, except instead of Eastern thought, it will be Eastern life. I want to be patient to let it come to me—never easy for me as you know, as our last phone conversations say so eloquently, so painfully to me as I remember them now. I want to be more patient than I was in Korea. I won't assume that everyone is ganging up on me just because I have no idea why in the hell they're doing something a particular way. I won't fly off the American handle. . . .

The "South Yard" of our campus, what I see from this balcony, is—like most of all of northern China that is not building, field, or road—made up of mud or dust. Now, after unusual rains the last month or so, the mud is packed hard from the wear of thousands of feet.

. . . After I stopped seeing you I met other women more easily—it's funny. Yes, they were younger. I remember you saying, "You need a woman, you've been going around with girls long enough." First there was Beth, lean and eighteen, ranked nationally in tennis, bored with private college, pals with the Kennedy kids, and wanting me to visit her family's place, a small palace in suburban Philly, that next summer. Her mother didn't know what I—not being Jewish or from the East—was there for that soggy July week, taking time off from my rhythm and blues band. Nor did I know what I was there for until Beth took off her shirt one night when everyone else in the family had finally gone to bed. The father, who was only a few years older than I was, was a ghost. The mother was

rich-prim and classy, but with a bulge in the tummy that even high fashion couldn't hide—three kids and too much ice cream.

"I hope you find whatever it is you're looking for," her mother said as they all put me on the plane a couple of days early. . . .

Should I not be telling you all this?

Xiao Zhang is leaving today. She is the cook's assistant. Very pretty, long hair tied back, high cheeks, quick smile, small waist, and round hips. When she spoke to me—only Chinese—her head would tilt slightly to one side, then the other, like a gesture of welcome.

I am told this had been for her only a part-time job. Many young people in China must wait for a full-time job. And now she is lucky enough to get one in a factory (as I think of her now, I can hear a morning whistle blow). As Lang Daying, our student interpreter, said, "She is not so young any more" (maybe twenty-one?) "and must take a full-time job if she can get it." She doesn't want to go, she says through him, but she must. I have to wonder, though silently, why she's not married, so pleasant and bright a disposition. Hers is another face that I could look at, could study for years. She says she'll come back for a visit.

. . . There'll be something else, some other force carrying me to the next day and the next, to the longer view, after which I can put down those binoculars all but fused to my face and say, "Yes, I'm alive now and there's nothing I can do about it." I plan to breathe more there, even if the air is bad. It's not so much that I'll come back a changed person as it is that I'll leave a person ready for change. Or maybe I'll come back and the whole American world will have changed around me, shopping carts become sacks of grain, lovers become wives and extended families, false hopes become children. Maybe it's that I'll come back. . . .

There's sunshine today, and it occurs to me now there was yesterday morning as well, for an hour or two, before the clouds returned. Perhaps this is the hour of the day to be standing here, seeing this scene in full, rare long light from a sun fighting its way through the coal smoke and fall haze that passes for a sky here.

Now a crowd of school children, boys, fifty or more, laughing and chattering, leaping foot by foot across the huge puddles in the walk. Where are they going? Where are the straight lines of Asia among all the punches and shoving of these boys? There are some slightly older boys along one side of the group, trying not very hard to keep order, occasionally sending a foot into the air in a mock karate kick to the one behind. They've all turned left, then right, back to the south, and headed behind the side of my building. This window is a north window and soon will be very cold. Maybe through winter I will watch, cold in the shade, the activity of those warm in the sun. But right now as the boys march off it is still an almost-fall day. The roses in the huge garden in front of our building have reappeared, the earlier blossoms knocked off, I am told, by the hail from last month's storm.

. . . I was surrounded by a sea of boxes, packing to move to a new apartment on the north side of Chicago, when a woman from New York called to ask if I was still interested in going to China. I'd forgotten I'd even applied—months before, in anger at some mishap at work. But by the end of the conversation she was saying how glad she was that I'd decided to go to Baoding, and that I wouldn't regret it. I didn't tell her I suspected no one else had sent in a resume, once again, as you always said, coming in first in a competition with myself. . . .

The garden is mostly mud, some morning glories climbing up the fence that surrounds it, some red flowers and orange flowers, like peonies, only Asian, around the periphery. Some bare fruit trees. There is a keeper of the garden who has a small house just inside the gate all to himself—paradise in China—surrounded even though it is by nothing, dwarfed by the apartment building and dormitory on either side looking down on his bare light all evening. I've seldom seen this man at work in the garden, and when I ask what his duties are, I'm told that he keeps people from stealing the roses. Just the other day, Gunther says, a man snuck in with a pail and shovel to do his beautiful dirty work.

LOVE, SEX, AND BICYCLES

A few months later we went one evening to an acrobatic show at the People's Theater, a live troupe from Shijiazhuang, just back from an Asian tour. They had a woman in the show who could lie on her belly and put her feet down flat on either side of her chin. At that point in the show a Chinese colleague leaned over to me and whispered, "Hundreds of ways to make love to her!"

This statement shocked me, not because of its prurient nature, since I had been thinking the same thing, but because it had been a Chinese who had made it. This was the first time that a Chinese had made any mention to me of sex. This particular man, though, had lived and studied in America, so I think it was my culture talking to me and not his. The Chinese seem never to talk about sex, and sometimes I suspect many seldom think about it.

I have a group of students, for instance, who are all former teachers come back to finish their degrees, so all are older than typical—twenty-five to forty years old. Of the twenty-one of these "Older Seniors" as we call them, all but three are married. Of those eighteen married, all but one live away from their spouses, some away from children, too. If such an arrangement were the exception in the society, we Americans would be amazed at their zeal in pursuit of knowledge, though we'd wonder about their hormone levels. But this arrangement is not rare.

Many married couples, especially the educated and professional class, live apart—not for months or even years, but more or less permanently. Even the husband of the president of our university lives in Tianjin—several hours away, and this in a country where travel is tiresome and inconvenient. The president tells me that she and her husband, a Party cadre, look forward to being together in retirement.

The government has said that the situation is regrettable, but necessary, since professional expertise such as these trained workers possess is in demand. But the real pity is that, according to Gunther, only about half of China's college graduates are working in their fields of study anyway. So the society has achieved the worst of both worlds—separation from career, separation from spouse and family.

And then there are those among my older students who live apart from their spouses even though they're living in the same town with them. "I live with my little girl," one Older Senior tells me, "but my husband lives across town with my parents because they are very old and can't take care of themselves." (She is quick to add, though, that the husband comes by during the week "if he needs anything," and then both she and her friend laugh out loud.) I ask her how old her parents are that they can't take care of themselves, and she says, "Almost sixty."

One tries to imagine such an arrangement working in America; one supposes that the marrieds could meet on weekends, but remembers then the close proximity of living conditions in China. Families of three or four in one or two rooms. Could Americans make love every weekend with their in-laws in the next room? In the same room?

I'd love to ask them about this matter—ask my students, that is, not the president of the university—but how can I broach such a subject when people give no sign of ever even thinking about it? Every day the evidence of their indifference confronts me. One day, for instance, playing ping pong outdoors we draw a crowd, which is to say I draw a crowd—a *waigoren* holding a ping pong bat the way he learned to down in people's basements in Wisconsin. Among the crowd, and among those who go whizzing by on bicycles, are women so beautiful that I want to pitch it all, throw in the sponge, and join the Party. As even Smith, my American colleague here, says—and he is a quiet, Ivy League sort—"Pretty women everywhere! And beautiful women are the closest thing I have to a religion."

Indeed, in China, there is a lot of everything human: beautiful women . . . and of course bicycles, which are human in that unlike cars they seem not to exist apart from their riders. I'm reminded of the Indians seeing the first Spaniards on horses, thinking that man and beast were one. Here, I see a huge parking lot of bikes and because of their uniformity—always black, always near the same design—they seem, apart from their owners, to have no character. It's only when they are ridden, tested out, that the differences appear—this one has better brakes, this one better tires, that one needs adjustment about the pedals or chain. This other is certainly newer, younger, liable to last longer. In China a bike may be livelihood—hauling a cart of cabbage, carrying a family of four. It is transportation in a country where many have never traveled more than a few *li* from their homes. And to buy a bike, one must wait and have about two months' salary, as well as a ration card for the better brands. Indeed, everyone has a bicycle, or wants one, or wants a better one. And by twenty-eight or so, everyone has a wife or a husband. Although the spouse is more important, and the Chinese know this, the bicycle may in fact be harder to acquire. Few think of improving their lot in that other way, few want a better wife or husband. To an outsider it seems sometimes that no one *has* wants of that sort.

For me in my Americanness, it's different. When these women ride past, young and beautiful—or worse, stop and stand and watch—my ping pong game, which is not up to Chinese standards to begin with, goes straight to hell. My serve goes flaccid, the topspin on the ball stops topspinning. What's the use, I figure. Isn't a lovely smile more important? A face? How can mere competition compete with art? And so much art to compete with, so much of all things human: men, but also women. And bicycles.

The Chinese, in contrast, don't seem to notice. Their ping pong game goes on uninterrupted. It's not that they are too involved in the game to notice the beautiful women. It's that they don't see them. If the players were sitting around only *talking* about ping pong and such women walked past, the result would be little different. No one would look up. Except me. The other day I hurt my neck while riding a bicycle and craning around to look at a woman riding the other way. The Chinese are spared such affliction.

Further evidence exists of what the American would think to be lack of sexual interest. My interpreter, Lang Daying, is a young senior student of mine, a bright, likable guy who wants to join the Party. He seems to be one who, we would say, is going to be somebody, and that's important here in the New China, as though the attempt at the elimination of class distinction made the differences between people—education, position—more important instead of less. Anyway, here is a healthy young man roughly the same age as these women I've described. One night waiting for a train I explain to him about cars and dating, what we did when we were his age and even younger. I'm naturally wondering about bicycles and dating. I know some of his classmates have boyfriends and girlfriends, and I'm curious. Had he ever had a date? With admittedly so many wonderful prospects from which to choose, doesn't he think about such matters?

"Maybe after graduation," came the perfectly honest reply.

I was to find out later that for a young man who wished to join the Party, this was the politically "correct" thing to say: the Party frowns on love affairs among undergraduates. But again I try to imagine such a situation in America. Even with bicycles we'd find a way, we Americans—a Schwinn equivalent of a back seat (though here the most popular make of bike is a "Flying Pigeon"). Cruising for action on ten speeds, down the main drag. Those gloved, perfumed hands tight around our American male waists as we pedal through the dusty night. Imagine the new possibilities for parking—places where even cars can't go. To borrow from the poet Robert Lowell, "The love bikes on the hill's skull, lined up spoke to spoke."

In China, are such scenes impossible because of lack of interest, or is there lack of interest because such scenes are impossible? The country has managed to make sex outside of marriage extremely difficult (as recently as the early seventies, says one author, people could be shot for licentious behavior). First, of course, there are the tremendous numbers of people (and bicycles) to avoid. Where are you going to go? Certainly not your place or hers. The fields? I hear it's done. But if you did find the odd hill or quiet grove, who, in a country where surveillance is considered benevolence, would see you? Since gossip here is as much a standard of evaluation as an entertainment, who would know? Who *wouldn't* know?

We're rehearsing a play in English for the student talent show— a just-for-fun thing, a short farce in which our interpreter Lang Daying plays a gruff but henpecked husband. The Chinese term for "henpecked" by the way is *qiguanyan*, which is a pun in Chinese. It literally means either "wife control strict" or "wind pipe infection." So if a Chinese man is henpecked, people just say he has bronchitis.

During my rehearsal Lang Daying is about to tell his wife that a painting they've kept in the attic for years is worth thousands of dollars. How appropriate, how funny, I coach him, if at the moment of discovery he would grab by the arms the actress playing his wife, look straight into her face and shake her in excitement: "Ten thousand dollars!"

The reply comes simultaneously from both my actors: "That's impossible." And neither will the bossy wife actress, my student and friend Li Fengyan, consent to bat the husband with her broom to get him out of his lazy chair. This physical contact is impossible too; I have to change my blocking of the scene. A bicycle, after all, can't be ridden upside down. No explanation necessary; it's just culture, that set of assumptions given to us which we can deny, but, try as hard as we might, we can't totally divorce ourselves from.

All this is not meant to criticize the Chinese way of going about things—of men and women, of love and sex, of bicycles. In contrast to the Chinese, we Americans have Madison Avenue: sex in advertising, in movies, and on television. We have our high divorce rate; we know that in our culture if you're still a virgin at sixteen (or is it fourteen now, or twelve?) you're a failure. Ann

Landers-types have for years been telling us about the errors of our psychosexual ways, and we don't listen. I think because we can't. Sex is part of our particular myth, our national thumb to suck. Given the American obsession with sex, the question becomes not how do the Chinese stand living apart from their spouses, but how do we stand living with ours? Or given my case, the question is not how do the Chinese live without thinking about sex and love every day, but how as an American do I live with thinking about sex and love every minute? How can I be American, single, and thirty-two all at the same time? Given that, how can I be living fairly happily in China?

At home, whenever I found myself becoming involved with a woman, panic set in. The panic was not over the good old modern American fear of entrapment (which is, after all, why we developed "relationships"—a kind of game where each player shares the assumption that the other is not necessarily playing for keeps), nothing that virile and romantic. My fear was, instead, that the woman would disappear. Because she usually did. I've reached this ripe old bachelor age, slept with more women than I care to think about, and never have I broken off a serious "relationship." I don't have to; they just end, like it did with Gwen. Or the woman ends them.

So I'm waiting for post-relationship America. I've come to China as a refugee from the sexual revolution, a boat person of the emotional and carnal. I made a promise to the exchange program that sent me here—hands off the girls (and they are girls here, even at eighteen, at twenty-two or twenty-three). "They get crushes very easily," I was told. "If you're expecting to have a Chinese girlfriend, forget it." When I arrived, on my first day in China, a dean at the university said the same thing to me. We were on the train to Baoding; I was busy culture-shocking, looking at China out the window. "Did Sharon and Edna tell you about the girls?" Dean Liu asked. He had lived in the States and knew our culture, our ways with things physical. "The girls," he said again. "Try not to get involved with them." This was the same man who was to later point out to me the variety of sexual positions possible with the acrobat from Shijiazhuang.

"A few years ago we had a Japanese professor who fell in love with a student. They were together all the time, and after her graduation, she left with him and they traveled together throughout China. It was scandalous. Soon they wanted to be married. Well, it was a lot of trouble, you can imagine. The government must get involved, the Party. There are a lot of papers to sign, forms to fill out. The family must give its consent. And now they are living in Japan, and we hear that the girl is very unhappy. We hear she misses her home and does not get along well in that society. It's very bad. So try not to get involved with the girls. It's a lot of trouble. It's not worth it."

As I look around campus I try to convince myself he was right, but there are so many arguments to the contrary. In fact if I had not taken a pledge, that would be the problem at hand—which *one* to get involved with. There is Guo Xiaoming, my tutor, but so many others. This woman is intelligent, beautiful, and fun loving. This one intelligent, beautiful, and articulate. This one intelligent, beautiful, and mature. Warm. Supportive. Curious. Aggressive. Self-assured. There are so many possible futures, so much potential happiness walking around in those different forms that to choose only one could leave me inconsolable at the thought of all I might have missed in the others. And all smiling, all smiling at me: "We hope to see you at the dancing party this weekend." "We'd like to come by your apartment to ask you some questions about D. H. Lawrence." "Would you like to join us for volleyball?" "For a walk?" "For free talk?" "Would you like to join us?" And each smiling, always, running up to me eagerly with something to say because I am the only person in the world, this world called Baoding, to whom each can say those special words. At least, say those special words in English, "We're glad you're here to teach us."

After a while I realize that a reason I came to China, came back to Asia, was, unconsciously at least, that I wanted this kind of attention from women again, what I got living in Korea, but what I seldom get in America. There, instead of visits and helping out, it's a need for space. Instead of smiles to smile, it's priorities to consider. Instead of compassion it's commitment—that's just our culture. I know it's not me they love, the Chinese, not for myself, but for my language; not my male difference, but my American difference. But I don't care.

And I know too the national anthem of American women is no more exclusive: "It's not you," they say, breaking it off. "It's me. I just don't want *anyone* right now." How is one supposed to answer that greatest of all American kiss-offs? If I hadn't enough character to make you want to stay, at least say I had enough to make you go away.

So I'm waiting for post-relationship America because I'm not very good at the serial polygamy our culture prescribes for the young (or once-young) and unmarried. I've chosen to come to China in self-imposed exile. Even with all the temptations around, all of the bicycles. So it was I was surprised to fall in love here. It was the day that I first rode a bicycle in China that I first made love in China. I didn't break my pledge; I made love with an American. But I rode bicycles with the Chinese—it's impossible not to. Snake-like streams of bikes flow through and around every city, so continuous that living here awhile you forget to see them, the way you forget to look for air even after it's wind and begins to move. Like wind, you notice only the evidence of bicycles, the care walkers take crossing streets, the worn expressions of some of the riders, the concern surely written on your face when you ride.

I carried her younger daughter with me on the bike that afternoon. I was naturally nervous—it was my first time. We set a pace to coalesce with the traffic around us, passing the ox carts and walkers in the street, keeping more or less even with the other riders. On the bike with Lauren, ahead of us, was the older daughter, and even the fact of the four of us, all blond, didn't draw nearly the stares we would have drawn walking. The other bicyclists had their appointed rounds to make. And riding, we whiz past those standing or walking—blond apparitions with a place to go, rather than just tourists, helpless and conventionally unconventional.

Those on the streets who did spot us no doubt thought me the father of the two girls, and well I could have been by the similarity of appearance—what to them must have made us look identical. I liked the feeling. It had been so long since I had been part of a family—even in this temporary way. In America, we do provide in a way for those who don't have families: in America we have taverns. In China there are few of what an American would call taverns, none in my town or this town where we biked. So we have families, or find one. I leaned over and kissed the back of the head of the little girl in front of me on the bar of the bike. This, I thought, is the success of having others around you to whom or for whom you needn't necessarily be witty, or skillful, or handsome or talented; needn't be a good lay or dress fetchingly. Not that in a family all these things cease to be pleasant. Just, I imagine, not necessary. Not all the time. What would it really be like? I imagine after a while forgetting to *see* her, just as now in China I forget to see the bicycles—the pleasure of taking a way of life for granted, of not betting all the chips on every hand. It's still a game, probably. But a longer game. You can lose some hands—it's OK.

We are pedaling faster now, outside of the town and headed for a temple in some nearby hills. I'm feeling more confident on the bicycle, balancing myself and the little girl, steering around the rocks and through the dust, keeping sight of the mother and older child ahead, or never leaving her too very far behind. I feel like we're drawing more attention now as we ride faster and pass the other bikers. The air, of course, is blue. I rush against its face. There are brown fall hills on all sides of us now—rather like eastern Montana, only with lots of people—and we're climbing so slightly on our way up to the temple. But below the dry hills are small farms—large gardens, really—lushly green with cabbage and spinach and beans.

The girl behaved poorly back at her home in the town—I wondered whether I could ever adjust to having children around, how anyone could adjust. They seemed just a small mass of selfishness, needing constant attention, forcing on me, with their crying and petty jealousies, a seriousness which I did not intend, forcing me to be something other than a child myself.

But now the same little girl, seeing that the precarious bike is no place for such bad behavior, sits very still. I talk in her ear, and she shouts into the air. We see the brown lives of the people, see pigs and mules and occasionally a tiny house with a roof weighted down by stones, with one bare light visible through a pane of glass, the only window. "How would you like to live there?" I ask. *What would it be like*, I say to myself. We climb higher.

The temple would have been a disappointment—as most tourist attractions in China are—if it had mattered. It was almost empty, and the caretakers played cards in the corner of one pagoda. The most amazing sight was a single needle suspended on a broken web from one of the pines that lined the walk from the main gate. Each breath of wind made the needle fly, and for the children I pretended that with my gestures and glance it was really I who controlled its pendulum motion.

That night Lauren asked if I thought Chinese people ever kissed. I said of course they do, but she said have you ever seen them. And so now as we kissed we wondered. I said that if they did kiss, they wondered how we could kiss with our big American noses. Surely they wondered about us, the Chinese at her college who knew her divorced and knew me unmarried and knew me visiting her. As we undressed we joked that her department chairman was listening, ear and glass to the wall in the next room. Or the students outside with binoculars, or with those x-ray glasses they used to sell in comic books in the States.

From the time I met her, Lauren reminded me of the older girls I had crushes on in high school, but now both of us older. "Eau Claire, Wisconsin," she'd said in a letter. "Small world . . ." She was a Minnesotan—practically a neighbor, the towns we'd lived in maybe a hundred miles apart. At home such distance, such separation is grounds for divorce, but viewed from the other side of the world, it's right next door.

I liked her more and more, and of course I would fall in love and knew despite my resolve that my own sense of need would leave me powerless against the attraction of the chance for a better life. In just the long weekend of my visit we had gone from being new friends to being new "friends." Sadly, I thought, this is often all that's possible for Americans in my time, this euphemism. I wanted my own cultural revolution, right there in the bedroom, that would allow us to be in love, to think of each other. But we didn't know each other, and I knew that and knew that my own feelings were sadly premature and bound not to be met by like feelings. Almost before we had finished our coupling could I feel her draw away from me back to wherever it is in our culture that we come from. Outside the window was night and China. Inside was just night. "It was good," she said, and she said she wanted to see me again. Despite the twelve-hour train ride from Baoding that made it impossible, I wanted to see her again, too, and so I smiled. But because the room was dark and because only the two of us were there, no one saw.

WALDEN EAST

◘ Why am I taking a flash picture of a young woman bending over a clay pot on an electric hot plate, stirring a vile smelling concoction that looks like what fills the spittoon at the local bus station?

Because I have to drink it.

The problem started when Smith, with whom I eat three times a day as if in an arranged marriage, complained of a fever and lack of appetite. When he missed lunch, I knew it was too late for me to avoid getting his cold. After all, if your dishes are given a cold water rinse after each meal, if Lao Fan, your cook, jolly and skillful though he may be, serves lunch with his thumb in your soup, you're going to get it, it being whatever everyone else has already got.

So now Miss Li Fengyan, my student and the reluctant actress in my play, is cooking for me some Chinese herbal medicine. "You must be very careful in its preparation," she says, making her point with the one chopstick she's using to mix the components of the brown looking stuff. "First, use only a clay pot, like this one."

The pot is rough like sand paper, and pieces of it crumble off at the touch. "Won't we get sand in the medicine?" I ask.

"*Mei guanxi.* It doesn't matter. The ingredients are probably a bit dusty to begin with, see? Anyway, we washed them, which should take some of the dust away."

We stick our two faces over the clay pot.

"What's in it?" I ask.

"I don't know the names of these things in English. I don't even know the names of some of them in Chinese."

"There's a piece of garlic . . . look, there . . ."

"Yes, and here's . . . what do you call this?"

"I don't know. I'd call it a . . . pod."

"And here's some . . ."

"Onion."

Italian food concocted by a terrorist, I think but don't tell her.

"Here's a kind of nut," she says. "Most of the rest is . . . roots. Roots of grass."

I'm disappointed but try not to show it. I thought my cold deserved something more uncommon, something in the eye-of-newt-and-toe-of-frog category. Panda gall bladder and some magic words. Despite the earthy nature of the stuff in the pot, I want to believe in it. I believe in it, I decide.

"You must be very careful in cooking the medicine. You must stir it only in one direction." She demonstrates. "Circular. Never back and forth."

"You must have enough liquid left," she goes on, "because after twenty minutes that's what you pour off and drink. Tomorrow morning before you teach your class you can cook the herbs again and drink the water again."

I notice she too has a cold, and as the smell of the stuff becomes more like that of a cleaning product, I decide maybe I'm not *that* sick, so I suggest we share the batch. But she says there wouldn't be enough, and besides, her mother is a Western doctor, so she herself doesn't believe in Chinese medicine. She says when she gets a cold she gets plenty of rest and drinks lots of boiled water.

She blinks her eyes once or twice. "If I get a cold," she says, "I just take two aspirin."

I've noticed that most Chinese, whether they take Eastern or Western measures against it, don't complain much about their colds. If I express concern for a student's illness, or selfish concern that I may catch that illness, the student just laughs at me and says, "It's a cold. It's very common."

Common it is. In this season when the weather's chilly and the heat's not on, easily one of every four or five people I meet has a cold. They say it's not serious, though they sometimes look terrible. The students just accept this time of year—the change of season, the coming of winter—as a time they're supposed to be sick. Sitting all day in an unheated classroom, eating unhealthy starchy food in unsanitary conditions, being crammed six or seven to a dorm room, the question is not how does one get sick, but how does one not? I'm hoping that it's all one cold that everyone has, or two, and that I'm through with it now, that it's not a series of colds that one might work his way through, antibodily speaking.

The stuff's done cooking, and we're trying to pour it out. It looks as if someone made a bowl of that party mix my mother always made from Wheat Chex cereal, and then left it out in the rain for a few days. Only it's hot. I offer what we had used as the cover to our clay pot—actually a broken metal light fixture I'd dusted off—to Miss Li as a plate to hold against the lip of the bowl to hold back the party mix and drain off the hot rainwater. She tries to pour slowly, but the icky stuff drools down the side of the pot and onto my desk top, soaking through a pile of sophomore papers and finally reaching my cassette tape of *Frank Sinatra's Greatest Hits*. I fetch a few copies of *The China Daily* to sponge up the sludge, then suggest she let me pour the rest myself. The old hand at pouring ice cream drinks that I am, I pour faster to dribble less. Only a few sticks and roots flow with the potion into my insulated cup.

"Very good," she applauds. "Now drink it while it's still hot!"

"Are you sure you don't want any?"

I hope to drain the vile cup in one draft, but it's too hot and I succeed only in burning the inside of my lip with a small taste. I sip again, grimacing. It tastes like some very strong coffee made from wood and candy bar wrappers. It somehow reminds me of the insides of the empty cans of Prince Albert brand pipe tobacco that my father used to leave around the house for my brother and me to play with when we were kids. I used to open them quickly to peek inside before the smell got out.

The truth is I'm not that sick. I had just wanted to see the inside of the health clinic on campus: the workers and students lined up in the dusty rooms, one poor guy dropping his pants to take a shot in the ass in front of all of us. I had been curious to meet Dr. Deng, the traditional Chinese medicine doctor, who for some reason when I first saw her was wearing a mostly-white smock as she stirred an electric wok toasting something that might interest a chipmunk.

Dr. Deng, Li Fengyan, and I then went into a larger room where people from the university work units were waiting to see one of a number of doctors, either of Chinese or Western medicine. My presence, needless to say, drew the eyes of all, even of a woman lying on a bed partly hidden by a curtain. She was taking acupuncture, and her body looked like a porcupine from all the needles stuck in it.

Dr. Deng took my pulse. Then she took the pulse in my other wrist.

"Hmmm."

Open your mouth, she said, and Miss Li translated. The doctor glanced at my throat from five feet away. She said it looked OK.

She asked about symptoms. Cough? Miss Li translated. Chest? Fever? By now everyone was watching the three of us as if we were talking an odd-shaped tennis match. I could follow some of what was said because that week I had studied in my conversational Chinese book chapter ten, "Kan Bing," or "Seeing the Doctor."

Then Dr. Deng asked about something else, and Miss Li smiled like a cat. All of the onlookers grinned. "What about, uhh, . . ." Miss Li began.

"No diarrhea," I said, and gave a negative gesture to Dr. Deng, who nodded in interest. Miss Li looked relieved.

We then went into a small room where Dr. Deng faced a giant cabinet that looked like the card catalogue in the Library of Congress. I counted more than one hundred drawers and noticed that each was divided into three compartments, each compartment containing a different herb or root or twig, a different component for traditional Chinese medicinal formulas.

Doctor Deng walked the row of drawers, grabbing a handful of this, a pinch of that, separating the portions always into two piles.

Then she smiled and handed Miss Li the packets of weeds, of nuts and bolts, that each looked like a Chinese nickel bag, and she related from memory the cooking instructions.

"*Xianzai zenmeyang?*" Miss Li asks me several days after I've finished the potion: "How are you feeling now?"

"Much better," I say. "It looks like that Chinese medicine really helped."

"Maybe. But Chinese medicine works very slowly. Maybe by this time you would have felt better without the medicine."

"Maybe. But anyway, it was just a cold," I say. "It's not serious."

Feeling better for whatever reason, I also feel a desire to take stock of my current state, feel ready to observe again the things around me—and the way I've changed, if at all, since coming here.

To begin with, there's my appearance: I'm wearing a new down jacket I bought in Beijing last weekend—bought, proudly, by myself with my infantile Chinese vocabulary. Underneath the down jacket is my *pi kanjian*, my old man's Chinese padded vest complete with genuine imitation sheep's fur lining. It's a heavy, bulky thing that gives me that Hoss Cartwright, let's-fence-the-lower-forty look, and, at 145 pounds myself, I like it. The shop where I bought it was an ill lit cave of a place with a faded picture of Chairman Mao on the wall above the stacks of real and fake fur facing the door as you come in. I loved the mothy smell of the place so much—right here in downtown Baoding—that I had to buy something, and why not this most Chinese of items? Never mind that no one under fifty wears such a thing here.

My pants are just pants. I'm of the opinion that pants, like underwear, should be nondescript. If a man's pants call attention to him, what can they be calling attention away from but his character?

Underneath my pants, though, lurk my *qiukou*, the Chinese word for long johns, which translated literally means "autumn pants." Such a term gives you the idea that winter comes as fast and early here as new love, and also that the people don't mess around with its severity. October, break out the autumn pants;

November, hoard cabbage by the cart load, by the Toyota van-load if you want cheap vegetables for the long dark season.

My feet are international: American wool ski socks covered by Chinese padded rubber boots with felt insoles added. The old-style padded shoes that made people look like they had to go to a blacksmith when they got out of bed every morning, those are rare as bound feet. Look for them on the very old. They're not available, and I find that tyranny. We Americans trying to pretend we're something other than what we are deserve the right to make our expatriate uniform complete.

So I'm wearing, in all, five layers upper torso, two on the legs ("Too thin, I'm warning you, too thin," says one old professor in my department, pinching at the clothes on my legs), three or four on the feet, plus a hat and some cheap driving gloves with holes cut in the fingers for writing (a Chinese invention, I think).

And did I mention? . . . I'm indoors.

It's 4:15 on a late November afternoon. I heard a rumor the steam heat came on Friday for a few minutes, but I was off to Beijing and missed it. I hope the vapor didn't see its shadow on the paved concrete floor and decide to crawl back into the pipes for six more weeks. In late fall in northern China, it's an Olympic-level sport just keeping warm, chipping ice off the intellect. The students—huddled up in their classrooms, freshmen and sopho-mores on the north side of the building, juniors and seniors on the less-chilly south—have given a new meaning to the otherwise bourgeois term, "overdressed." The students have slowed to nearly a stop, too, this time of year, their shyness replaced as an excuse for not talking by a penetrating cold that turns bones to hoarfrost. We're all waiting for that clank from the radiator—the way the first American colonists must have awaited mail from England.

Of course, as a "foreign expert," as they call us, I have privi-leges not allowed others, indeed not allowed by law: my apart-ment is heated, one of its four rooms at a time, by the twelve hundred watt hot plate upon which Li Fengyan cooked my medi-cine. It's the kind that transients in America use to cook meals in cheap hotel rooms. But even the hot plate is of no use when we have no electricity. Lately, it's been going off almost daily from mid-morning to night, which suggests to me others are using hot plates as well: Party cadres—the privileged class here now—and an occasional lower class person surreptitiously "cook the air," as my students say. The circuits are overloading, and as a result sometimes no one has power.

It's 4:30 on an early winter afternoon here at Walden East. The sky is going from light gray to chalk gray, more serious about its grayness. Here at Walden East the pond's been drained for irrigation. The trees are all poplars, which grow like weeds, their cold leaves spinning like streamers at a windy car lot. There is beer, thank God, good beer, and there's no problem keeping it cold without a refrigerator. Keep your tea cup cupped in your hands and your beer on the floor next to those two blocks of ice, your feet.

Needless to say, with this kind of cold, with undependable power, hot water is also not to be counted on. Every night from seven to nine we're supposed to be able to take showers. Right in our own homes—by Chinese standards an unthinkable luxury. But for Americans, those untempered by a month or two here, the knowledge that the water may start at five or end at eight, or not be hot or even warm enough to avoid a chill (my shower window doesn't close completely), or not come at all may subvert peace of mind on a dark afternoon. But then showers themselves become less necessary. Not that we stink here—our diets change, and there are less drastic means to avoid B.O. than self-immersion. Taking a shower every day or two becomes as silly as changing clothes every day. It's only American foolishness that keeps us from wearing a shirt for five days, isn't it? And why shave often? Why shave? I'm thinking about a pony tail for the first time since the sixties.

It truly wouldn't matter here. Or as the Chinese say, "Mei guanxi."

Here in my personal Walden, there's no TV or obvious means of entertainment, either. True, I brought back some newspapers and news magazines from Beijing, but I'm not anxious to read them. News, it seems, like everything else, so they've been telling us all this century, is relative. With no paper on Friday, reading

Thursday's paper, or last Thursday's, or last month's isn't so urgent. There's no chronology, no progression of stories: hostages taken, hostages threatened, hostages released. Dewey defeats Truman, then Truman defeats Dewey. *Mei guanxi*—it doesn't matter.

Even mail becomes subject to this time lag. The problems discussed in Aunt Mary's letter three weeks ago are no doubt solved by now. Similarly, the subject I so passionately describe will be history in a month when Gwen asks me about it in her reply as though it happened yesterday. Smith and I figure it takes a week for letters to get from the States to Beijing, then another week from Beijing to Baoding, 150 kilometers and fifty years away. (Time travel, it seems, is a slow business.)

Mei guanxi.

The bomb shelter decor of my apartment doesn't matter much. That the place reminds me of a basement, that with bars on the window it could pass for a jail doesn't matter. That the walls are poured concrete, whitewashed so that you'll chalk your coat if you lean against it, doesn't matter; that the floor is an unpainted gray version of the walls doesn't matter.

Mei guanxi.

When you've been in a place for even a short while you begin to learn a few phrases that aren't quite translatable. *Mei guanxi* doesn't mean "it doesn't matter." It means *mei guanxi*. Indeed, *mei guanxi* seems to be used not only for dismissal or condolence, but as statement of my opinion about what you want or your opinion about what I want. Smith and I approached Lao Dong, the Director of Foreign Affairs, one evening: "Won't it be cold in our apartments until the steam comes on?" "*Mei guanxi*," he told us. Then he told us stories about how he fought the Kuomintang without even a blanket. As we left, he gave us each a frisbee. "How can you expect me to teach if I can't get my textbooks?" I ask the librarian who's locked them in a room for cataloging for several months. *Mei guanxi*," comes the reply.

In this society, for the Chinese, what an individual may want truly *doesn't* matter. "I would like to work as an interpreter." *Mei guanxi.* "I would like to be able to read and say whatever I like." *Mei guanxi.*

For a foreigner, the effects are not so constricting, and in fact after a while may become liberating instead. That my apartment has the decor of a cold bombshelter truly *doesn't* matter, because the furniture is very comfortable. When the sun shines through the south window it's quite cozy. And maybe there *will* be a bomb. *Mei guanxi.*

We can't drink water out of the tap, and of course that doesn't matter because we have *kai shui* through most of the day. I've come to like it a great deal and think even when I go home to the States I'll keep a big red thermos of boiled water at my feet. The loudspeakers that blare propaganda, "news," and exercise music wake us up each morning at six A.M. whether we like it or not, but that doesn't matter because we can have our nap, our *xiuxi* every day after lunch.

Chinese workers have the right to *xiuxi* written into the Chinese constitution, so important is this practice. During *xiuxi* the campus is deserted for one to two hours, longer in the spring, I'm told. If I start my class before 2:30 some afternoons, I'm greeted by a classroom of bleary eyes and short attention spans. If I'm traveling, trying to run errands or make purchases in Beijing, I find this black hole in the middle of my day a disturbing waste of time. But here at Walden East it's the most peaceful time of day. There's a comfort and reassurance in the practice that we lack in the cells of our lives in the West. Here, like the dirt on the walls of the dancing hall, the cells are real; they're where we live and sleep, not the space buried in the shell of our own bodies where no one is allowed. Alone here with all these people, I'm less lonely than I am in my own country, even taking my nap alone (the outsider wonders how many children are conceived after a good lunch). Here I'm not expected to fit in perfectly, and, happily for everyone, I don't. There, in America, I'm expected to fit in, but even not fitting, find tremendous competition. There are so many individuals in America that it's hard to be successful at being different. In America, some conclude that the only way left to be different is to waste their lives or go out and buy a gun. All the other ways have been taken, been thought of already.

No mail, no heat, no light, no water at times. And at Walden East, no philosophy either, not for the expatriate. The Chinese have their homes and lives; their hopes, individual and national; they have their friends, their language, and, although they don't think about it, their culture. For the foreigner comes the wonderful freedom of not being a part of any of that. There is no common philosophy except in his past. He's not accountable, doesn't need necessarily to be consistent with what he's done in that past. A person can quit smoking or start, or do both every week. Pray to a god or not. He can pray to a cigarette—or more often, a drink. He can cry. Ironically for the citizen of the society that offers more freedom than any in history, if he leaves that society for a time there can come an even greater freedom—the delightful freedom to just be, to try on a new character, like a new set of clothes, modify the old one like a fine car. I write in a letter to Gwen that one of the joys of being in China, of being at Walden East, is the liberating feeling that none of this really counts, that I'll take up real life in America again, with all its hassles and crap, soon enough. In that greatest of all American metaphors, no one's keeping score here. Life is an endless exhibition season. Spring training. A benefit concert sung for your own cause. *Mei guanxi.*

Gwen writes back, "It may seem like you've learned nothing in your travels, but you have, after all, learned to survive." I may become proud of this the way a soldier may be proud of what he's done in war even though he doesn't like war.

JIE ZHENGUO

▣   The year is 1938, and the Japanese occupy much of northern China. In Tangshan, in Hebei Province, a coal mine is all but shut down by a series of strikes led by the heroic members of the Communist Party. The British manager of the mine is in a quandary about what action he should take to reopen the mine in order to continue to feed the Japanese war machine. The manager is a heartless capitalist owing allegiance to no country, to no one but himself. His response is to "make an example" of one of the leaders of the strike, who has since, of course, become one of the people's heroes in China and thus is a fitting subject for a five-part Chinese television mini-series.

I play the evil British manager.

I was cast because of . . . what? Good looks? Natural talent? Or because there are only two foreigners in Baoding, and Smith recently had his head shaved to take a Chinese medicinal herb cure for his dandruff? If you forget I've never acted before and consider that I don't look Chinese and thus make a convincing foreigner, I'm perfect for the part.

When Lang Daying, my student-interpreter and the husband in our play, told me about the plan to make a TV show in Baoding and told me that I would have a part, my first question was why the hell anyone would come to Baoding to make a TV show (unless it was a trailer on donkey shit I thought to myself). The reason, I found out, is that Baoding has some buildings left from 1938, the year the story takes place. These particular ones are not beautiful, but in general such buildings are rare in China; the Japanese leveled many of them, and the Cultural Revolution leveled more.

The TV crew is from Tangshan, Lang explained; Jie Zhenguo, the national hero whose life the film depicts, was from Tangshan, and the events of the film take place there. But Tangshan today has no buildings older than 1976, the year that whole town was leveled by an earthquake.

I remembered hearing about that particular disaster on the evening news in the West. I've since learned that Chinese lore says earthquakes precede a change of dynasties. Months before this one, Zhou Enlai died; within months after it Mao too was dead, and then the Gang of Four was overthrown.

The government says the Tangshan earthquake killed 148,000; Western sources say 800,000. I asked Lang why the government would lie about the number of people killed in an earthquake, and he said that the Gang of Four didn't want Westerners coming to China to help out. I've noticed that if you don't like something here, it's proper to blame it on the Gang of Four. So when my shower didn't work, I told Lang that I suspected, even though they're in prison, the Gang of Four. I was glad he got the joke.

Now, of course, as the *China Daily* tells us, the government is following the correct policy about things. Then why do they still lie about how many were killed in the earthquake? I'm not sure, and I don't ask Lang about this one because I know he'd feel he had to explain the inconsistency, and I don't think his English is quite good enough to explain; I don't think anyone's English is that good.

My total screen time on Chinese television would probably be between five and six minutes, Lang told me, but to shoot this much—partly because of my amateur status, I suspected—took all morning. I think from that morning I learned more about TV and movies than I did about China. What I'm saying is that such projects may be similar anywhere in the world. To me, to one who speaks so little Chinese, and to one who saw the cast and crew for only a few hours, its members seemed to be trying to fit the stereotyped impressions of movie people that we Westerners hold.

The director, for instance, wore a scarf and a funny beret with his Mao suit (Sun Yatsen suits, they call them here). He was handsome and hard working, and jumping all over the set to give cues and explanations. When he'd tell me what he wanted me to do, the presence of the interpreter—not Lang or one of my students, but a woman especially assigned from city government—made things wonderfully more confusing, and consistent with the buzz of activity around a movie set—just as our imaginations would have it.

And there was the script girl, a little bit of a thing in a permanent and bobby pins with a ready smile for me, a *"hao le"* and a thumbs up when we'd gotten through a scene and my "performance" had been OK. I could imagine she was having an affair with a sound man, almost as if I were home and watching television instead of here and being in it.

There was the makeup girl—short and pudgy in her flannel shirt and jeans. There were the nameless guys with the boom mikes, and other nameless guys with lights and cameras who would take turns screwing up so that we'd have to shoot a scene six times because somebody's shadow showed up on the monitor, or because the cigarettes the prop man gave me to fondle were filter tips . . . in pre-war China. There were the machines of every sort that took turns not working so that I had to be led away to a warmer room for the pneumonic cough I've developed this winter as a result of that cold I caught last fall. "Please take a rest," my interpreter told me while the crew was trying to sort out the most recent malfunction.

The guy who played the foreman of the mine, who played opposite me in my several scenes, was a popular Chinese actor. He had been in a movie I'd seen only the week before and had been in the Italian production of *Marco Polo* that played on American TV some years back. He was rugged and handsome and fifty-ish and seemed, again, trying to fit into the stereotype we have in American films of the slick Oriental tough guy who's going to punch out Sam Spade or Indiana Jones. Such is the nature of the People's television. But in the flesh, the guy moved so gracefully, big as he was, so confidently, so in control of every . . . eyebrow, while I felt myself twitching away as I always do, as though my heart pumped black coffee from a truck stop off the Interstate. I learned from him, a two-hundred-pound Chinese, what I lacked besides beauty that would keep me from ever becoming an actor: body control.

And the actress, the one who played my secretary: obviously cast for her long and slender looks and hair down to her thighs. She'd float onto camera, lean over and ask me in Chinese what I wanted. "Miss Yang, I want you to make a phone call for me right away," was supposed to be my reply. . . .

And then there was the People's Hero, the martyr Jie Zhenguo. In the story I have him killed. But in the filming we had no scenes together, so I never met him.

I had only a small speaking part in the show, but I was confident that I'd get some great lines because, before we began shooting, my interpreter and I just made up the lines. Everything I would say would be dubbed over anyway; only the gestures and expressions need be appropriate. In the finished product, my lips would move to the voice of some evil Chinese baritone—a technique reminiscent of "Mr. Ed."

There were a couple of places where the situation and the gestures dictated more exactly the content of particular lines. For instance, after a long walk down a corridor with the Chinese foreman of the mine (shot in three separate segments; everything in TV is in idiot-proof, bite-sized takes, I discovered), we come into the cold light of day, and I stroke my beard the way bad guys do and ponder, "There must be someone *behind* the strike. . . ." very pregnantly, and of course the TV audience has known since 1949 that it's the Reds who are behind the strike in the mine, and I'm just figuring it out today.

I loved every minute of it, loved the lack of the understatement that we're told is the rule for TV in the West. Everything here is clenched fists and knit brows. Shouts and whispers. At one point I got to jabber away angrily on a phone (I could have been reciting an order for pizza and beer for all the crew knew), hang up the phone, pace back and forth in silence and then say, "Damn."

"Cut cut cut cut cut," the director says in English. And then through our interpreter: "but we need something longer—say more angry words."

And so on the next take I bang the phone down, pace, then let out with a "Damn it! Goddamn it!" And again, "Cut cut cut cut cut," or something like it, this time in Chinese.

Third take: I slam the phone down so it bounces off the hook, throw my arms in the air and, having by this time recited every word I never said in elementary school, begin the list over again until my face turns violet, setting off my evilly pompadoured blond hair. By this time into shooting, some of my students who've heard about what's happening have biked downtown to watch and are behind the floodlights. I finish my "lines" and look up to see Lang Daying and Li Fengyan—my thespians—and Guo Xiaoming and some others all grinning broadly at my performance, not at the naughty words, which I doubt they could follow, but at my display of emotion. After the take there is the obligatory moment of "quiet-on-the-set," then a roaring round of applause.

Several months later my students and I begin to check the TV listings for notice of "Jie Zhenguo." On the week that it is broadcast, I invite them by each night to watch. A special invitation is extended for the final night, the episode into which most of my five-minute appearance will be spliced.

I have my apartment ready for a big group, having stopped at the street market for several *jin* of peanuts and at the special foreign export store for the only chocolate in town that doesn't taste to me like paraffin. I have, cooling in a tub of water in my north room, plenty of beer, a treat for the students (the cost of what I've bought equals for most of them an entire month's government allowance). I even cleaned the place, swabbing what is literally a rag mop over the porous concrete floor, making the dust fly off my desk and tables with an old shirt before it settled back again pretty much where it had lain.

The evening begins as most do with such a large group. The three students who've been accepted into the Communist Party—Lang Daying; Xie Rong, a bright woman who's a senior; and Sun Je, a student I don't know well—sit together on a couch, slightly separate in bearing as well as location from the ten or twenty others. The eating and drinking comes first, as is the fashion here, then the guests settle into paging through my collection of English language magazines. Later on, the crowd will thin out, maybe I'll bring out more beer, and the less straight-laced and more adventuresome of the students will loosen up. We'll laugh and talk more, sing some songs while I honk on the pump organ in my living room. I know among their favorite songs is "Silent Night," and that the Christmas season is over makes little difference. They find tremendously funny that line at the end where the melody slides up a major third, singing it in a loud, exaggerated way, giggling happily afterwards: "Sleep in heavenly PE–EEACE." The party might go on this way until well past eleven, when I will maybe walk the girl students back to their dormitory so the attendant will know where they've been and let them in without getting too angry.

This evening, though, the anticipation of the group is for the climax of "Jie Zhenguo." I've invited the whole damn town over, I think, for five nights of waiting for the ninety seconds to see Professor look like a popsicle stick (or ice sucker, as they call them here) on provincial TV. Even the part-time workers in the slum-like dormitory next to my apartment building have been following the series, the one worker with a TV having put it outside in the courtyard where all can gather after dinner.

Finally somewhere in the second half-hour my big scenes appear. One student is ready with a flash camera to try to take for me a picture of the picture on the screen. The spectacle of me before the hundreds of thousands of viewers of my province is not disappointing. I can't dominate the screen like the foreman of the mine, or float across it like the woman who plays my secretary, but neither do I after all look like an ice sucker. The nature of television and of the narrative is such that I appear, in the week of drama, in the splicing and cutting between scenes and places, inconsequential. In fact, one student who went back home last week, to Tangshan, saw the series broadcast there, not knowing that I would be in it and not entirely sure that I had been: "The hair . . . Teacher, your glasses missing . . . you appear so . . . white." In my brief moments of stardom the thing that I notice most is my suit. I had to wear my own, and it is hardly a 1930s period piece—a blue blazer, Pierre Cardin, thin lapels. I am probably the only one in Hebei Province to notice this.

But one can surely do worse: to become among even this portion of China's masses—those masses being a concept that has become in English though not in Chinese a cliché—inconsequential. To somehow blend in, to be invisible, to be a part of something you were not by birth, or the random humor of geography, or the calculation of politics, meant to be.

"You have great emotion," Lang Daying, the Party leader among the students, tells me, and the others agree that I was right for the part.

TRYING TO BE INVISIBLE

December 15, 1985

Last week's snow has all but melted. A dusty gray lies in the north shadows of walls and buildings, much like March in the American Midwest. Walking, I've turned down a small *hutong*—alley—with its mud-brick houses, lined up wall to wall, each uneven and irregular. Their bricks seem piled on top of one another as if the wind could blow easily through the cracks and into the rooms. The houses look temporary, as if they were set up for refugees. But the red metal plates tacked to each and bearing a number address tell me they're indeed permanent. In the courtyards of the houses, also encircled by bricks, are wash basins, hanging laundry—the things of life. On one house I can see newspapers pasted around the front windows. I can hear a dog bark, which surprises me because dogs are illegal in the city. In places where there are no houses there are more bricks, stacked high.

Suddenly a pack of children tears from around the corner wall. The littlest ones are dressed in a wild combination of bright colors, a contrast to the drabness of ordinary citizens' dress. The coat of the smallest child hangs down below his knees, and his sleeves hang a good four inches past the end of his hands. This way, one assumes, the coat can be worn for quite a number of years before it's outgrown. The children are playing a loud game, and they run back around the corner without spotting me. If they'd seen me they'd have shouted "foreigner, foreigner," which would have brought more packs of kids from around more corners.

I've turned across a mud and stone bridge over a ditch with water passing slowly underneath. I'm surprised that the water has little smell and think it's because of the cold weather. I look back for a moment, and the twilight emphasizes the colorlessness of the domestic landscape, the gray-brown growing black. I notice that above each brick hut rises, long and spindly like the backbone of some dead metallic animal, a TV antenna, silhouetted against the sky. For the Chinese this is a proud sign of modernization, and the contemporary paintings in the museum in Beijing now feature, along with the usual tractors and factories, scenes such as this one—rows of old houses each topped by an antenna, a mark of progress.

I haven't been down this alley before, and I'm surprised that when it ends at a junction with a busier, paved street, I'm in a small free market place. There's a crowd of small carts that blocks the intersection, but this doesn't matter because no cars will turn down the mud alley anyway. On each cart a candle glows, its wick a metal pipe leading to a pot of oil at its base. At each cart a peasant is hawking goods, and one peasant grabs me by the arm and points out that the bread on his cart is packaged in plastic—almost as in the West. He himself is wrapped in a blanket against the cold, wearing an *ertou*, or ear cover, a kind of open knit stocking that hooks over the ears and passes underneath the chin like a woolen beard. These articles always look funny to me, the way they make the wearer's ears stick out like some small elephant's, so I stare at him as I pass, and he stares back at me.

I see carts of apples, carts of oranges and pears, carts of peanuts and, the students' favorite, sunflower seeds. From another cart a man is selling candied crab apples and oranges, skewered together on sticks. Each stick juts out from around a center post and in the candlelight the transparent sweets glow red and yellow. Another vendor pulls a blanket from over her cart as I pass, and as she does, steam rises from a pile of *mantou*, the hot steamed bread that substitutes for rice in northern China. From another cart, mostly enclosed in glass, steam is rising off red meat and dark organs, liver and kidney. I can also see the breath of people in the night air and the breath of resting horses. Most of the shoppers are on their way home from their work units at this hour, picking up a few things. There's an air of great activity about the place. But at the same time, this free market, this symbol of modernization and reform, suggests, strangely, an image of the Great Depression in America: a line of ill-clad people spending all day and evening over little more than a pile of apples.

To one side, over on the walk, I see a crowd, which usually means in China an argument or a street showman. Sifting through to the inside of the circle of people, I see a man with a red blanket spread on the walk. He's talking almost non-stop, and it looks like the old shell game: two red beans magically disappear from underneath the cup on the left and reappear beneath the glass on the right.

Stand back, he tells the children crowding in. Now, "*Chashui*," he says, holding up a glass of tea. He talks without stopping, describing its obvious qualities of color and heat. Then he places a magic card over the top of the glass, dips in one dirty index finger and as he talks on, the color of the tea turns from gold to deep, dark brown. Then the card and the dirty finger, and again as he talks the gold color reappears. The children remain captivated, but one by one the adults disappear like so many red beans. As they do, others appear at the front of the circle to take their place.

I watch a long time, but never does he collect money, never does he gesture as if he's trying to. The beans appear, disappear, and reappear. The onlookers do the same. Now a deck of cards, and the steady stream of words continuing. Still he takes in no money. I'm puzzled, but also cold from not moving in the night air. Back at the college I could ask an English-speaking Chinese how such men support themselves. But I decide instead to come back tomorrow and watch him some more.

Dear Gwen,

Another juke box Saturday night in Baoding. This week I traded my Pat Metheny tape even up to Smith for the White Album, and sent him Bach's Suites 4 and 5, for Bartok's Concerto for Orchestra and a composer to be named later. I've had my shower and poked myself with my allergy shots. It's 9:35 and I'm ready for bed. There's no dancing party tonight because there were two this week to celebrate the New Year holiday. But I was sick, and so I missed them both.

Yesterday the wind blew so hard the inside doors in my apartment wouldn't stay closed, even with pieces of cardboard stuck in the cracks. The wind blew the newspaper stuffing right out from the quarter-inch gap around the window in the can. I went outside, and the sky was red and grainy from dust, and there was one—what can I call it?—long slide of dust like a road going into the sky to the south and west. It looked like Mars outside. It looked like the sky was growing. The whole effect gave the usual gray-brown monochrome of this place a kind of red sepia tint. It looked, it even felt like it should be summer, except that it was very cold.

Maybe it's Venus, not Mars—a tintype tint in the sun, and not a blade of grass anywhere: they pulled up the last of it by hand during the Cultural Revolution because Mao said grass was bourgeois. The land is packed hard clay, like at the bottom of a kids' slide in the park, or underneath the merry-go-round. There is mile upon mile of such landscape, which looks, above all, very tired. Or maybe the weariness is mine. But it seems, given the bleak drabness of this landscape, given the cowtown nature of even Beijing, that, as far as northern China is concerned, somebody's airbrushing a lot of tourist literature. People who come away talking about the beauty of China are seeing what they want to see, are judging the book not by its cover, but by the price of the taxi to the bookstore. China is fascinating, but for one reason only: because it's China.

The days are getting longer. When at 6:30 A.M. the tinny, distorted exercise music with its accompanying yi er yi er—so that the whole damn world knows it should get up at the same time, which means less trouble for the bureaucrats—when that political grocery store music begins to issue forth from the M*A*S*H-like loudspeakers all over campus, it's at least begun to get light. Similarly, when we stagger from our drafty classrooms at 4:30, stop in the mailroom, and head out into the orange last light of the afternoon, there's at least light, though the lack of its duration and the cold and wind of what I'm told is the coldest cycle of *the winter here have put an end to the after-school volleyball, badminton, or even tennis that I've come to enjoy.*

I've learned that one can be the best tennis player in town by being the only tennis player in town. In a town with two rackets. I call them "the clay courts," though they're really meant for volleyball. We just roll the net on one of them into a single wide strip and play you have to hit the ball under it. This game only proves that things are very different here, though not necessarily in the way you expect they will be. There still are many things I don't understand—about China and about myself—but maybe understanding's not as important as I thought it was.

April 8, 1986

The other night from my apartment I counted the lighted windows in the boys' dorm: twenty-five windows across, five stories high, so 125 rooms on each side of the hall. Multiply this by seven students per room, and you've got seventeen hundred plus kids living in this one building alone, which Smith refers to as "the hive" at night when the lights are lit.

Tonight, one of the first warm evenings of the spring, I decide after filling my thermos bottles to walk just a few steps out of my usual path and find myself standing in the middle of the large packed-mud courtyard between the two largest dormitories on campus, boys in one and girls in the other. I can look inside the lighted windows to see how the students live. In rooms no bigger than a dorm room at an American university—and maybe smaller—are four bunk beds, seven beds occupied, and one upper bunk used for trunks or suitcases. Occasionally as I walk I see some rooms with a guitar or small radio. And because of the shortage of space, towels and clothes are hanging from the ends of the beds or from hooks implanted in the concrete walls. The scene does not look like that in a jail, but only because jails are not this crowded. The smell, even from outside in the courtyard, is of piss. Someone, somewhere is playing an *erhu*, a traditional Chinese two-stringed instrument with bow. A few stars are out, and the air is calm and black.

Once or twice students have taken me into their dorm rooms,

somewhat reluctantly because of the crowded and dirty conditions. But this experience tonight is different from those because I knew those people; those rooms were filled with conversations and familiarity. This night, from outside looking into the lives of strangers, I find the effect is much different. The light, for instance, is different—the bare fluorescent lamp that lights all rooms in China I've ever seen, including my own. But from out here in the dark, it seems to remind me that I'm living in a country that's not my home. It seems sad in a way I can't explain. Maybe it's the sensation of walking past room after room, seeing the life inside, but also seeing the walls between the rooms from a point of view those inside don't have. It seems to give me an unfair advantage over them, something like the advantage I have observing their culture from the vantage point of my own.

I have by this time looked across the yard toward the girls' dormitory. But more of the curtains are drawn against the night, and I'm farther away so I can't see in well. The girls, I'm told, live only six to a room instead of seven, evidence of what in America young women would cite as a favorable on-campus ratio. In China this doesn't mean much. From what I can see the rooms look the same as the boys'. There are more clothes hung up—maybe that's international. And then I notice the big difference of curtains—more like sheets—that can be drawn around each bunk. The girls probably draw them for privacy when dressing and undressing. I'd wondered about this; I couldn't and can't imagine a room of young Chinese women stripped one before the other. And I still wonder how the bathhouses are set up.

This lack of space and the resultant lack of privacy it brings people may help explain why many Chinese I know don't confide in others easily. Living so close together makes gossip too great a force to discount. Just today, for instance, I noticed that Jiang Xia, one of my favorite students, had been looking very unhappy, and this was the second week in a row she'd looked that way. I asked her if she was feeling all right, and she replied that something was bothering her. This was more personal a confession than I'd heard from anyone the whole seven months I've been here. I was surprised, but I tried not to show it and said in a teacherly way that she could tell me about it if she wanted, after class. I knew that this would likely never happen, and she seemed to respond by acting happier and perkier after class that day, as though she were concerned not about how to confide a problem, but with the fact that her depression had been so obvious. How different we Americans are, and how much this experience here makes me act American: for instance, asking Jiang Xia, someone who would rarely confide in anyone, if she wanted to confide in me. That's very American. It's a kind of harmless showing off of how open we are as a people and how little we think gossip and self-revelation can harm us because we don't care—or maybe because we don't live six or seven to a room.

I pass some large lecture halls and stand outside the window and watch for a long time. One lecture is being delivered by a man in suit and tie—maybe Chinese literature class?—and another by a woman in an army suit—this may be math or economics. What one really sees from outside, though, is the crowd in the room, all the dark heads from behind, the restlessness. Not rare is the sound of someone spitting on the floor, and then his or her head rights itself again. The students seem quite attentive for the late hour, and the scene suggests to me a primitive version of those classrooms pictured on American television appeals for money: give to the college of your choice, or some such thing. Again I feel the advantage of the peeping Tom, but less so because these people are busy with something that I definitely am not a part of.

I also stand before some of the quiet, mostly empty night class-rooms where students retreat from those busy dorms in the evening for further study and maybe for some degree of solitude. This is the Chinese department, I think, and I am standing so that I can see into two rooms at once, with the wall in between. The desks in one room face away from those in the other, as if there were no wall and the occupants were somehow trying to ignore their neighbors, reading quietly, heads down, in the next room. I see that in one of the rooms one of the glaring fluorescent lights is out, so those in the back row are maybe squinting, faces low over their books. Somehow I feel here like a painter who is, by seeing this, creating it. I want to carry this plain sight on with me the way one carries the memory of some great personal event, a death or a feeling of love or embarrassment.

Lately in my letters home, especially to Gwen, I've been growing more and more political, and I don't like it. It's as though faced with the politics around me I feel I have to swim strongly upstream. This night makes me think maybe the repression of this system is not totally to blame for the listlessness, the helplessness I sense in the people here—especially the young, like Jiang Xia, my quiet student with something bothering her this morning. I'm thinking tonight that maybe the listlessness is related to the rooms I peered into tonight for moments at a time. Some of it may just be numbers—numbers of rooms, of desks, of people.

As I head back to my apartment I pass the single rooms all in a row of the part-time workers on campus. They do construction during the day, and at night they live in what we'd consider conditions akin to camping. The shelters are brick tents as to their amenities, with bare bulbs. The back windows I pass are very high, like transoms, and I can't see inside, but I can imagine. One guy has a bottle of clear booze set against this the north window. I stop and crane my neck.

The lives of these part-time workers in their rooms are clearly the dimmest to me, more limited even than the lives inside the rooms of the students. Back inside my apartment and looking from my own window, I can see the one tall TV antenna, still shiny and new, rising high from above the room in front of which the workers gathered to watch my TV show. And where other nights they cause us such annoyance. The new color TV set is placed in an open window, and all the workers in the courtyard gather to watch—twenty or thirty of them. The problem results because of the Chinese predilection for music and dialogue at what for me are ear-splitting volumes. It's simply not loud enough unless the speakers are buzzing and distorting. There's little concept of bass or fullness. To my ear, it's not in their classical or pop music, either—not in the lovely nasal falsetto of *Jingju*, Beijing opera; not in the few Chinese rock bands I've heard, which didn't even have a bass player.

I remember on an evening similar to this one watching the group of workers push up the long bamboo pole, two or three times as high as the roof of their dwelling itself, on which the sacred TV antenna is mounted. *Yi, er, san* . . . , they grunted, and then pushed the wobbly stick up in unison—once, twice, then again, and the third time it stayed and they shoveled enough dirt around its base to hold it firm. If Americans would say these workers are just like Americans, in front of their TVs at night, then those Americans would be wrong.

Beyond that, it's better for me to reach no conclusions. Maybe we come to strange other-countries so as to be unable to draw conclusions and thus put that very active censor inside ourselves to rest for a while. I look as I look at a lot of stars on a very clear night. They're not, finally, bad or good, right or wrong. They just are. That I can do nothing about them is a relief as much as a fact.

TRYING TO BE
A TOURIST

◻ I admire the professional traveler types, intrepid young people with backpacks, who choose to ride the rails in China by hard seat or hard sleeper, essentially second class passage, in order to "see what the people are like." But seeing plenty of people in Baoding and travel being tough enough in China for me, I try on a train to get the best seat I can. To me, hard seat—as opposed to soft seat—means that for a few dollars less than the fare for being comfortable I can bring on board thirty kilos of luggage and several chickens as most people seem to, then do a fifty-meter dash with the load to get the last place on a hard bench before someone else does. Hard sleeper is a compartmentless Pullman wagon with three bunks floor to ceiling (instead of two as in soft sleeper), a kind of interment for the living that makes me feel like I'm inside a candy bar. So it is that during the long spring vacation which precedes Chinese New Year, when I'm bound for Shenzhen and then Hong Kong on the two-night train ride from Beijing, I make sure I have my soft sleeper booked well in advance.

As this train pulls away into the night, into my compartment come three jovial men about my age. I thought there were no Russians left in China, but the language these guys are speaking, they and six or seven of their friends buzzing around the train car, is indeed Russian. They're instantly friendly, my compartment mates, and before we even introduce ourselves they hand me a can of Coke. One of them looks to me like Alan Arkin; another pudgy with a smooth, feminine Nikita Krushchev look; the third, who can speak a few words of English, short and kind of pimply, fair-skinned in an eastern European way. He wears blue jeans that say "Texas" and a pair of ankle-length cowboy boots. Krushchev has a cap that says, "Sport." We talk some, and though we don't solve the disarmament question or banter about Afghanistan or Nicaragua, neither do we accuse each other of undermining Chinese self-determination. One reason the conversation is limited is that the main language we have in common is Chinese. This leaves me at a tremendous disadvantage—maybe the way our conservatives feel at the negotiating table with their conservatives—since they have been studying Chinese here full time for several months while I haven't.

But are these my enemies? We can say little to each other, yet enjoy it rather much, so that it occurs to me that political answers to international problems lie perhaps not in more dialogue, but less. Maybe we can solve international differences if we make our leaders speak to each other in a third language they don't know so well—so that they can't say anything to each other more sophisticated than "Would you like some tea?" "Try a piece of this bread from Beijing," "Please," "Thank you," and "Good night."

By the time the train is passing Wuhan, a day into our journey, such conversation as is possible between us has lapsed in favor of long periods of reading and napping. From the window I can see that Wuhan is another Chinese city where the principal colors are gray and brown. It's 2:30 in the afternoon, and, having left Beijing last night at 10:30, I've yet to see out the train window much that I would call beautiful. The color of the world outside the train is so dull I want to think the window glass is tinted, but it's not.

It's very difficult to order thoughts on sights seen from a train window because the images flash by so quickly, almost the way the mind itself works. A few minutes ago, in the countryside, we saw the roofs of houses weighted down by bricks—as though shingles or nails had never been invented. Now, coming into

Wuhan itself, we see the somewhat neater dull red tile roofs, which inspire more confidence that the inhabitants underneath could stay at least dry, although perhaps not warm.

We cross a tributary of the Yangtse—green in color, as are many rivers I've seen in China—and then the Yangtse itself, wide and brown, as though it must be too shallow for navigation. But defying this sense are a few boats that leave a white wake on the surface of the brown, giving the appearance that the water is covered by a surface of oil. Above the surface lies a layer of fog and, one assumes, industrial pollution, for this is a Dickensian city in the midst of a Dickensian country. I wouldn't be the first to compare the look of modern China with the average Westerner's notion of early industrial revolution England—coal and smoke.

I left Baoding yesterday with the promise and the hope of seeing something beautiful. I was hoping, too, in the passing cities, to see something more personal, more identifiably Chinese than the wide, cold, impersonal avenues of Beijing. I was told that even though this is January, south of Henan Province I'd see a green landscape again—which I've barely seen since I arrived in China in September. Significantly, I was told so by people who'd never been south of Henan Province.

How to think about hundreds of millions of people—or just my students, for that matter—who have never seen anything other than this? What does the word "beautiful" mean to them (and what do "freedom" or "democracy" mean)? This plainness and industry, this soulless repetition of gray cubes and misshapen huts, this alternation of dry land and barren mountains—this is the field from which my students must determine what they consider to be beautiful. Fate and nature have played a cruel joke on them, placing so many people in this one country, this one place, making that place lack the resilience, after thousands of years, to accommodate them.

I consider the fact that my student Guo Xiaoming, the dancer and my competitor in the running backwards race, has never been even to Beijing. Her entire experience is shaped by Baoding and the countryside. Yet twice since I've known her she's turned to me and said over some small good fortune, "I'm so happy!" And she was.

The first occasion was a New Year's Eve dinner with her classmates. After one or maybe two glasses of wine and a few *jiaozi*, the Chinese steamed dumplings served on special occasions, she turned to me and said, "I'm so happy," probably from the alcohol, which girls seldom drink here, and from the warmth of the occasion. I compare this party with the debauchery that accompanies a weekly or, at some points in my life, daily series of drinks at the local saloon in my home in Wisconsin. Is it that we Americans don't know how to enjoy ourselves? Is it that we know too well?

Another occasion for Guo Xiaoming's happiness was receiving a form for application to graduate school—actually it was a review sheet with sample questions for the admissions test, certainly not acceptance to the school itself. She has a pixie-like face and haircut, a manner that she herself admits is youthful. She has energy and pep. This school for which she would study endlessly to attend was in Harbin, the coldest major city in China, where summer exists in someone's imagination for a week or two every July. Harbin. Home of the Ice Festival. Home of ice. "Oh," she said in her quick way. "I'm so happy!"

I don't resent this happiness, this innocence; it's just the teacher in me that's disturbed. Sometimes I think I'd like to take Guo Xiaoming to the edge of the Grand Canyon and say, "Look at this. No one lives there." Or to the Lake Shore in Chicago, and say, "This is a city." Or even to the typically overpopulated small lake in northern Wisconsin where my family has a rundown cottage— a lake plagued by too many motor boats and by too few fish. We'd row to the middle, look at the evergreens, the birches and blue sky, and smell the air. I'd say, "This is where I live."

And then I'd like to have her describe it for me, in Chinese. It wouldn't matter if I could understand the language or not. I'd just want to hear the tone, see the face. Then I could imagine what her experience would be like: to discover, at age twenty-two, this other physical world. To prove for me that it's still possible to have previously unimagined experiences in life. How could Guo Xiaoming have any such concept of beauty as I would show her? It would have to be a complete surprise. "*Oh, I'm so happy.*"

The extrapolation is that such experience awaits the rest of us as well, if not an experience of the beauty of landscape, then of some other kind of beauty, or of some concept other than beauty, previously unimagined by us. Perhaps love, then, is possible. Possible in the gray streets of Wuhan. In the socialist dreck of China. Or is there some other emotion waiting, previously unimagined?

"In our church, we can speak freely, here in the presence of Jesus Christ," the small man says.

Then he drops to one knee to pray, facing the lined and cracked painting of Christ, surrounded by unlit colored lights like those an American family might string around their picture window in December, here hanging above a makeshift altar. The man invites me to try the small pump organ in the rear of the plain sanctuary, then I follow him out of the church to the courtyard and on to the parsonage to have tea with the bishop. The exterior of the church, built by the Hui minority people in this remote small city of Dali in Yunnan Province, must be unduplicated outside of the region. It looks at first like a Buddhist temple in its shape, with its tiled roof and swept, curving lines. But missing are the Buddhist murals and iconography, the figures lined along the eaves. Atop it is a cross.

Dali itself is a small city located ten hours by cardiac-arresting bus through the mountains of western Yunnan Province from Kunming, the capital. The week I visited was the first that foreigners could arrive without a travel permit, but even by this time Dali was becoming popular with young travelers. Unlike much of the China I had seen up to this time, the China that I thought of when I thought of Guo Xiaoming and my other students, Yunnan Province is a truly beautiful place, and Dali may be its most interesting city.

Populated largely by ethnic minorities, Dali sits beside long Lake Erhai, the clear blue color of which is best appreciated from somewhere on lofty Cangshan ("Azure Mountain"), which rises from the other side of town. Because of the clean lake, the high mountain, and the diverse population, there's quite a variety of things to do and see in Dali. Perhaps enjoying the outdoor setting is a key to the charm of Dali. Most who have never been to China don't understand what an environmental disaster much of the country is; Dali is not like that. There is as much to see and do outside of the town as there is in town. The hiker or even the walker on Cangshan gleans the pleasure of looking back, of being *away* from a place from which he set out. He even has the pleasure rare in China of doing this without crowds of people around.

But neither is Dali some rugged park for the misanthropic foreigner. People provide the other pole of attraction of the place. Two gates stand at either end of the village; you can walk or, as a matter of fact, see from one to the other. In between is a long main street filled with shops selling marble or jade objects to visitors or selling provisions to residents. There are also a number of Hui minority restaurants, since there are in Dali a large number of Hui people. Originally from central Asia, their skin is darker and their eyes rounder, their faces less perfectly round than Han Chinese. Indeed, at times the sight of an old Hui woman or young boy on the streets gives you the impression you're in any country but China—Burma, Thailand, or perhaps Syria, Greece, eastern Europe.

The Bai minority is in fact the majority in Dali—the girls and women in their bright colors not as a tourist show, but for daily wear. Bai men can be dressed in any odd way—rags, blue jeans, "traditional" Chinese army clothes, even dress that's Western to some degree is OK. But Bai women seem to us foreigners dressed as though they're going to spend an evening at some exotic Halloween party. They wear pink and red and orange, right along with deep blue and green. The colors are displayed on a tunic, with a wide sash around the waist, and on a headpiece worn in such a way that the woman's hair is braided around it, twining the rich black with its bright colors.

Mr. Chang, the small man of the church I have stumbled upon on a sidestreet of Dali, is of Hui nationality, but is obviously a devout Catholic, whereas most of this group are Moslem. Chang speaks English and French fluently in addition to knowing Latin and, of course, his native Chinese. There are 150 Catholics who attend mass at his church, he tells me. But between here and the western frontier of Yunnan Province with Tibet, there are perhaps 8,000 Catholics. There had been more than four hundred churches to which they and many others had belonged. But that had been before the Cultural Revolution. Since then only four, not including this one, had been rebuilt.

"C'est un traviste," Chang says of the Cultural Revolution. We have been joined in the bishop's room, dusty and damp with a large table in the center, by three French travelers. There are some new bicycles on one end of the room. It seems the church receives only a thousand *kuai* a year for leasing some of its buildings to the government for use as a middle school. Now they hope to rent bicycles to tourists "at a lower price than the hotel and restaurants" in order to raise more money. They have two young men studying at seminary in Kunming and desperately want to keep them there. To make the package more enticing, Mr. Chang offers to accompany us or any other travelers on bicycles to a mosque and a market in a neighboring city in a few days, perhaps some weekday morning after mass.

Now the bishop is pouring hot water for tea. My glass has enough leaves in it to serve everybody in the room, and the leaves stay floating near the top of the hot water so I can't drink without them clinging to my lips. The bishop looks monkey-like with his long black and silver hair sticking out over his ears, which themselves stick out. His upper lip is broad, his hat pulled down close to his eyes. He's wearing a long black coat over a blue Mao suit, and he reads silently from a book during the whole conversation that follows. He speaks and understands only Chinese (and of course Latin). He is easily seventy-five years old, perhaps eighty, and appears to nod off to sleep from time to time.

I think I'm the only one in the room who understands French solely on the basis of three years' training in junior high school. Mr. Chang goes on to tell us—according to what I can make out and what is translated for me—of the horrors of the Cultural Revolution, about how much of the town was destroyed, about the persecution faced by Catholics and other believers—Protestant, Buddhist, Moslem.

"In our church, here, we can speak freely in the presence of Jesus Christ," the little man had said with a half smile, and then he prayed. I feel a chill of realization that this had been an authentic experience, that his words embodied the old idea of church as sanctuary—a place where one can speak away from the repression of the central government. The Communists profess granting religious freedom, of course. It was front page news in the *China Daily* when the old Catholic cathedral in Beijing was reopened in time for midnight mass last Christmas Eve. What's not said is that Catholics must take an oath of allegiance to the country in order to worship, and under no circumstances is the church allowed to take direction from the Vatican. Because of this, mass in the church is still said in Latin, the altar faces the back instead of the pews—basically none of the reforms of Vatican II have been instituted.

Mr. Chang was proud to describe his acquiring of English and French proficiency. He found teachers, he said, in whoever passed by, learning French from Swiss, French, and Belgian missionaries; English from missionaries and later American servicemen who'd come to supply the fight in the anti-Japanese war. The Americans had had an air base near Kunming built for them by the Chinese, through which they supplied the resistance (Kunming being on the Burma Road). At one point, Chang told us, he was to go abroad to study, but because he could speak the three languages and was the only parishioner in the area who could do so, the church said it needed him in Dali. In Dali he had remained a lifetime.

He'd had for years no opportunity to practice his foreign languages—in which his skill was impressive even now—until Dali opened up to tourists a year ago. Old Chang makes us guess his age before telling us with delight: sixty-seven.

"And so," he concludes, "I can say in my life I had no teacher, and I had many teachers."

The peaceful half smile remains.

If the Chinese are not so observant as tourists one has to wonder why. It's certainly not because they're blasé about the process from overindulgence and overexposure, given the long work week, the almost non-existent vacations, and the general tendency of the Party to deny people, especially in the north, any but the smallest pleasures in life. Maybe the casual attitude toward sightseeing is because the Chinese know that tourist attractions that have been around for two thousand years will likely be here tomorrow, so why get excited? Whatever the reason, if the Chinese seem rather uninterested in looking at sights, they display far more enthusiasm for looking at people, especially at Westerners.

Theirs are not the stares of the thoughtful or amazed. They seem to me the empty stares of the openly curious, yet also colossally bored. I ate lunch the other day next to a man straddling the bench on which I sat, sitting so close to me I would have been able to count his fillings if his mouth hadn't been filled with partly chewed rice and green vegetables that he dribbled down his chin out of interest in me. This staring surprised me because I've noted less of it here in the relatively easy-going south.

In the north, if two Chinese are having an argument, usually about the price of goods on the free market, a crowd will gather to stare. Not to take sides, but just to stare, each head shifting from side to side. If two bikes collide, or if a bike hits a pedestrian and some yelling ensues, a crowd will gather. Seldom will an onlooker offer an opinion on who's in the right and who's in the wrong; there's only staring. If, in the middle of winter in Baoding, a horse has fallen in the icy snowy street, and if that horse is struggling to get up again, struggling to pull a heavy load of metal pipes, or scrap metal, or bricks, and if the master of the horse is beating it with a whip to get it to stand and pull and work, striking it repeatedly and hard, a crowd will gather in the falling snow, hands clasped behind backs, to stare. This is culture, and we can't understand it. It's dangerous for us to pretend to understand. It might be bad for our minds, our psyches, our personalities, our souls. Most of all, to pretend to understand a culture you don't is disrespectful.

One day after I return to the Kunming area from Dali, I find myself in the parking lot at Shilin, the Stone Forest, a tourist attraction for Chinese that the guidebooks claim is overrated. Going there anytime around Chinese New Year, the one time families are reunited and the Chinese take from a few days to two weeks off from work, can give any Westerner the feeling of being in Asia—it's crowded. I had wandered there along the stone paths and steps among the giant "trees" of limestone that had been weathered into strange obelisks, not at all uninteresting. But back at my bus in the parking lot of the Stone Forest, I saw what was for many the real attraction.

In one small tour bus, a Western father, middle-aged, sat with a badly crippled, deformed girl. Her legs were like two sticks, bent at the bony joints. Her knees were wider than her calves, wider than the thighs above the knee. Her arms hung stupidly. Her mouth hung open. I had seen the two, along with a wife and one or two other children, walking the touristed paths of the Stone Forest earlier in the afternoon. "Jeez, to bring that kid all this way to the other side of the world," I'd heard another Western tourist say in admiration. The father had carried the handicapped child— not a young child, not a baby—up and down the stone walks, narrowing and widening between and among the stone trees. I had tried not to look long.

Now inside the bus the girl lay back in her father's arms, head against the window. I could see in the light through the tinted glass that he was dabbing the dry gums of her open mouth with a damp cloth.

Outside, at the front of the bus, a group of ten or more Chinese men and women, boys and girls, stood pushing and elbowing each other—as they do at a bus stop—craning their necks to get a better view of the deformed girl (and one wonders were they also looking at the father?). An old man lifted a little boy onto his shoulders for a look. *Kan yi kan,* to have a look.

I couldn't look long, but I saw the young father's look. He was a handsome man with straight hair and a broad face. His look was full of patience and full of fatigue. I had to think he wished the starers would go away for the child's sake and not for his own. His was a simmering look. But a resigned look, as those who live with handicap—their own or others—wear. When I stare myself, I try to be invisible. So I felt disgusted at the Chinese, whose motives I couldn't understand.

This is culture. The father and girl are culture. The staring of the Chinese is culture. The onlooking American is culture. Above all his sympathy and disgust are culture. The reactions are too quick to be reasoned or educated away. If culture is taken away, we are left with only eating, sleeping, lust, excretion. We are left with fear, maybe with worry about the future, maybe with concern for children. Maybe not. We are left with self-concern.

This is why I believe those who try to change cultures will never succeed entirely, and they should realize this if they want to live as well as they can in the new or different culture. This is why I think those who try to deny their culture—especially Americans abroad, because America, for better or worse, has the world's most seductive culture—are fooling themselves.

In Shanghai, one night a few weeks later, I closed up the Peace Hotel Café with its jazz band. A trumpeter led two saxes and a rhythm section—one violin lost in the back—through a selection of pre-liberation era standards. Only the trumpeter on an occasional lead, or the better of the two sax players when he switched to clarinet, played around with the melody at all. No one "took a chorus" in the American sense. Improvisation is not big in China; what's more, one Australian resident of Shanghai told me, you can set your watch by the order of tunes the band plays every night.

The bassist, like the two soloists, was quite good—playing in tune, playing in time. The other players dropped a beat here and there, blew flat, or missed changes in the tradition of old-fart wedding bands in the American Midwest. But together, and especially considering the setting, they were entertaining as hell. The people in the audience—all foreigners or "overseas compatriots," as the Chinese call people from Hong Kong or Singapore, or Chinese Americans—loved them. This despite the tender age of most of the "backpack travelers" in the audience and despite the fact that even some of their parents were young enough to have turned up noses at similar Lawrence-Welk-done-badly back home. It's understandable. What at home is plain or corny becomes novelty in the rarified cultural atmosphere of Asia, of China. One breathes harder for things Western here, and the ventilation can be dizzying.

The band was well into its second hour before I heard a tune that was post '49, post liberation. "Love is a Many Splendored Thing." Not long after that came "Strangers in the Night" and "Spanish Eyes." Some of these "current" tunes must have been snuck in through Hong Kong, the same way that high cadres bring in videotaped pornography. The rest of the band's charts probably survived hidden away under someone's mattress through the fifties, sixties, and seventies.

If that explains the music, what about the musicians? Who within a system where it's always a good idea to say nothing when you have a good idea, suggested, "Hey, why don't we have some of the old guys in town blow Western tunes six nights a week at the Peace Hotel Café? The tourists will probably like it . . . and spend a lot of money on drinks. . . ." The Australian resident told me the players were "refugees from the Shanghai Symphony. They can make more money working here." They were sixty-ish—meaning they were in their mid-twenties when foreigners were last ensconced in sinful Shanghai. They had good memories, I told the Australian, to remember what these tunes should sound like after forty years.

A Glenn Miller medley sets the crowd clapping. They cheer wildly at the close, yet I am the only one yelling "Pennsylvania 6–5000" at the appropriate moment, underlying my point that the crowd's enthusiasm is more for the milieu than the music. And why not? The trumpeter probably doesn't know they're ap-plauding for the wrong reasons, and he probably wouldn't mind anyway. He counts off an Ellington tune, then "Autumn Leaves," and then—can it be?—"I'd Like to Get You on a Slow Boat to China." The irony's lost on the young travelers.

I plan to go up to inspect the saxophones during a break, but the musicians never take a break. The violinist plays a few tunes solo with rhythm section at one point. And one guy hauls out a Hawaiian pedal guitar. That's the only rest any of the musicians got. Don't tell the union . . .

The band is the new craze here, the Australian tells me—and though I think he means Shanghai, he really means China. People in Shanghai, Westerners and Chinese alike, tend to view their city the way New Yorkers or Parisians do theirs. "What else is there?" they ask. "What else that matters?" One can imagine Shanghai stores selling variations on those New York maps of the U.S. that show California just west of Philadelphia. Here it would be Shanghai City, then Beijing in some polar region near the Great Wall, and then somewhere upstream on the Yangtse, Europe.

The Hawaiian guitar is a little slippery for me, and the sliding produces strange, unplanned key changes. Or maybe it's the drinks. The menu contains at least fifty selections under each of two categories: Western cocktails and Chinese cocktails. Something about a list like this just invites the foolish traveler—especially one on holiday from the reaches of northern China—to start at the top of the list and drink his way down, in more ways than one.

Having proceeded down the list, I duck out ten minutes before closing time in case I have to get a taxi. But first I ask directions, in perfect Chinese, for the bus stop. The reply is also in perfect Chinese, and at a speed which, even sober, I couldn't understand a word of.

And so, too proud to admit my ignorance, I stagger out and find the bus stop by instinct and what I remember of the bell hop's hand gestures. It's still raining—has been for my whole three days in Shanghai—so I stand underneath my umbrella, feeling vaguely British Colonial in the streetlight. One bus whizzed past while I was on my way up to the stop, so at least I know I'm in the right place. This is the north end of the Bund, Shanghai's main drag. It's still way early enough to be the same day it was when I started out the evening, yet around me is mostly silence. There are some others under other umbrellas—even couples, a welcome breath of liberal change from stodgy Beijing. They talk a little bit, but not much. There's no wind, so the light rain is coming straight down, making it relatively comfortable to stand here. Only my feet are wet, shoes soaked through from two days sloshing through the puddles and the streets. But I've been drinking and so, though I notice, I don't care. There's only the rain and the streetlight, an occasional car or taxi or bus. It's been a long time since I've had this much to drink. Socialism presents one, especially a foreigner, especially in Baoding, with few good reasons to stay up much after dinner. To get drunk in the third world, in Asia, is an experience I recommend highly. And to get drunk in Asia if one hasn't been drunk in a long while is even better.

This is not Baoding, but Shanghai. City of opium, prostitution, British astringency, and French *joie de vivre*, vertical city of class and classes, structure and infrastructure. And city of the past, for when I climb on the bus, well before midnight, the shops and restaurants we pass on Nanjing Lu are all closed, metal fronts drawn down over the storefronts in Asian fashion. The city looks like it's boarded against a typhoon, only instead of wind there is merely night. It occurs to me that this is what Hong Kong may look like by 2010 or so—the look of Europe, the people of Asia, the lifelessness of Communism. Hong Kong with its shopkeepers—selling goods of all varieties—gone home. Still, visiting Shanghai for a short time, one sees the European façade, the 1930s feel of the concessions. What a difference between this city and the sterility, the coldness of Beijing. For one thing Shanghai has . . . beauty, character, architecture. And don't forget that ingredient missing in almost all Chinese cities that I've seen: trees, the color green. Finally, to compare Shanghai to Beijing is like comparing Greta Garbo to Big Nurse.

The conductor yells at me when I reach my stop. I've still got a few blocks to walk down the lamp-lit, tree-lined streets to my hotel. I want to relish every step of it. Such an easy, guilty pleasure, the kind gained before midnight. There's an occasional couple passing, a single man on a corner. We're all under our umbrellas, shoulders hunched, hands in pockets.

Staying at an elegant-by-Chinese-standards hotel in Shanghai, I have occasion to observe more Western tourists, particularly American, than I have at any time during my stay in China so far. I find it a less than reassuring experience. At breakfast the next day, for instance, I am amazed at the arrogant way people use the words, "hey," "coffee," "yes," "thank you," and "no," as though they were part not only of some international language, but of some shared culture. Nowhere in this collection of sport shirts,

pot bellies, and wide women do I see any evidence of people acting like guests in someone else's country. I doubt their way of
looking at the world will be changed a great deal by their coming
here.

Most people from any country who come on a group tour are
probably very nice. But there's something about saying, "Do you
have any syrup?" that strikes me as so ignorant. The concept of
syrup doesn't exist here, as far as I know. It seems to me that in a
foreign country, if they don't have syrup on the buffet table, you
should assume they don't have it. Isn't the fact that they even
have a "buffet" table enough for you? After all, that concept
doesn't exist here either.

I hear one overweight woman say to another overweight
woman that she ordered chocolate ice cream last night and got
vanilla ice cream with chocolate sauce. Doesn't she know that
Mao wanted to replace all restaurants with rice dispensaries? This
is important to me because I'm wondering if I, in my constant
complaining about Chinese politics and bureaucracy, sound like
them. I'm reminded of the very pleasant Mexican woman I met
on the plane here. After telling her my fears of visiting Mexico
and running into anti-Americanism, she said Mexican people
weren't against Americans. They were just against people who act
like assholes.

I've now seen most of the major sights in Hangzhou, the place
that, along with Suzhou, the Chinese liken to heaven on earth.
I've been underwhelmed by many of the sights, mainly by the
tourists that crowd every square centimeter of land designated as
scenic. I'm surprised, though, that these tourists are not of the big
nose variety, but are almost entirely *Chineseus holidayus*. It's fun to
watch their posed pictures, especially the girlfriends and new
brides—calendar-like, hand on hairstyle in front of each sculpture
or glade of flowers. It's fun, but a little sad, too, which is why it's
so interesting.

I've been to the temple in Hangzhou and climbed hills, biked
the causeways that run two ways through large West Lake, the
main tourist attraction here. I must admit that, toward evening
when the Chinese group ethic has dictated the time for sightsee-

ing has ended, the lake has a kind of allure. Perhaps it's the allure of water in quantity, anywhere, the blue-green smell. Perhaps it's the swallows.

And now I've found a little spot, not far from where I'm staying at the university. It's called Jade Spring, worth about twenty minutes of tourist time, and maybe half a day for the traveler, sitting around, sipping a beer, reading a book, and taking in the stillness.

There's a small pond here, circled by a walkway and a few benches, and that circled by a garden of trees and shrubs, all greener than an ad for menthol cigarettes. Brightly colored flowers—lilies and azaleas and others I'm too ignorant to know the names of— fill the woods.

What strikes me about this place is design and scale. There's a simple pagoda-like structure at one end of the pond. Almost anywhere else around the pond you can see it reflected in the water, which has brightly colored fish in it. The pagoda on the pond has moss and grass growing from its roof. The pagoda is bordered by a bush, flowering white, which picks up the white of its exterior walls. There's also a red-leafed tree—like a red maple in the States but with different, more Asian-shaped leaves—at the side of the pool, matching the red of the pagoda's roof.

Right now, evening, some people still stroll the walkway. A guy down the path to my right is standing with an open sketchbook and pen. I look up at him and catch him looking up at me. Across the pond from us is a young couple on another bench, the man in a sportcoat with his head in the lap of a young woman in a neat yellow suit that looks to be made of a very soft, soft material.

Are the two of us on this side of the water writing about and drawing the same subject fifty meters away, on the far side of the lake, closer to evening? I can begin to hear crickets, tree frogs, and the happy sound of night frogs around the pond's edge and off in the damp grass. My beer's almost gone. The artist has closed his sketch book, bumped his kickstand, and strode off with his bicycle. Now, if no one has run off with mine . . .

After traveling a few weeks, I find myself becoming numbed by the succession of people, events, and scenery. I remember, for instance, in the Western Hills near Kunming, scenes of beauty I would have killed to see in plain Baoding, but which I only notched into an unwritten travel diary in my head. This in turn makes me continue to wonder about those professional travelers, those with backpacks off for a year or even more. How, after a few months, do they prevent a spectacular sight from becoming just another peak, just another temple?

I had such an experience in Fuli, a somewhat remote village near Yangshuo, which is itself less touristed than nearby Guilin. I enjoyed the primitive narrow streets of Fuli, populated as much by chickens as people, enjoyed the inactivity of the populace, the hanging meat drying on wires that ran from house to house and across the narrow lanes. At one point a man walked past with a goiter dangling from his neck, big as a breast. Biking out of Fuli, I heard a clatter of small voices. I was puzzled, only to find they came from a gaggle of school children, crowded on a corner, waving me a loud good-bye.

Despite these sharp images, later that same day, someone back in Yangshuo asked what it was I found interesting about Fuli, and I couldn't tell him. It had all gone. Out the back of my head. This is what happens to me when I'm gone away too long. I stop seeing. I lose my capacity for amazement. A donkey cart is just another donkey cart. The third world becomes generic.

In another sense I've been going away all my life—seven jobs in eight years in three different countries, never more than twenty months in an apartment, never more than two and a half years in a town at one stretch. I've never renewed a lease in my life. Gwen wrote to me in a letter something like, "Sometimes you have to go away in order to come back again." She was talking about a psychological distancing from friends and environs. But what I've done is to go away physically—first from America, more recently from Baoding—so that I can go back again.

Now maybe I'd like to start coming back. Maybe first to Baoding, then to America. Maybe to friends, home, a more normal life. More than ever I think it will be these "regular," conventional things that could make me happy, or less troubled at least, over a long period: someone to sleep and eat with, a bearable job with lots of free time, a bowling team, a weekly volleyball game, seasons, regular friends, a place to fish.

Mostly now, thinking of home, as I'm beginning to, I find I miss things that aren't really there. Today I walked down the Chinese street and broke into a smile thinking about the poker games I used to hold in my basement. The Chinese passing stared at me even more than usual as I walked along alone, laughing out loud. I feel like I want to go home and have a poker game and invite my friends from high school. The problem is that they're spread all over the country, and they have wives and children, have lives. And when we can get together in spite of all this some odd Christmas, it's never like it was.

So what I miss is not the States, but, since I have no home, no life there, I miss the past. I'm an expatriate of time, not physical distance. I've separated myself from a remembered reality— pieces of different times and places—not from a geography or a politics or a culture that happens to be my own.

How does one become repatriated with his past? To what, to where does he return?

The artists and writers of the twenties and thirties felt they couldn't work in America, so they left it. They couldn't live an artistic life there—which is to say for them that they couldn't live any life. I didn't make a life for myself in the past, and so time moved on. Without making a conscious decision to do so, I've abandoned the America I belonged to. In a sense, certainly without choosing, I've abandoned everything but myself.

THE SPACE
BETWEEN PEOPLE

◻ The Chinese are people who American pop psychologists would say do not have good "body awareness," telling us in the TV-talk-show kind of way that says more about Americans than it does about Chinese. But I don't think the Chinese would care much about our notion of body awareness. I doubt the term even exists for them, and if it did it would carry an entirely different meaning.

This is not to say that Chinese people are physically unfit; the close attention that many Chinese pay to exercise predates the fad that's gripped the live-forever sweatsuit set in the States. Totally without health clubs and how-to paperbacks, Chinese culture has managed to popularize jogging and exercise—to the point that dawn is one of the busiest times of the day for foot traffic.

Exercise, like dance, has the blessing of the Party: if people exercise, they will be healthier and can do more work. If they do more work, they do more to modernize China. But even the elderly are caught up in the craze, which leads me to think maybe the tendency to exercise is a matter of culture rather than politics. Once in Kunming, for instance, on my way to catch an early bus I walked the streets past the park in pre-dawn light. Not more than twice arm's length from each other stood old people, each facing the park's lake—about every third one with a transistor radio blaring pop music or the morning news—and each doing some form of stretching exercise, some form of *gongfu* or *taiji*. They were lined up there, none paying much attention to me, each repeating the strange movement of arms or legs—like so many awkward sea birds that have been affected by some marvelous pesticide. As they stretched and turned, other elders in sweat suits jogged in the streets at a pace just slower than my fast walk, but with fists clenched and arms cocked at the elbow in the posture of a runner, feet shuffling.

This penchant for exercise is evidence of the "body awareness" the Chinese seem to have. But living with a lot of other people in a small space and living in that space poorly, the Chinese allow for a different definition of what is an acceptable distance between these bodies. One can easily see this on crowded buses, at ticket booths . . . in fact almost any place where in the West there would be a line, in China there's a crowd. Two different Chinese friends have told me that one thing that impressed them upon coming to America for the first time was the orderly way we Westerners stood in lines.

Even at Shilin, the Stone Forest near Kunming, one of the Chinese' most popular tourist attractions—a huge place with the capacity to hold dozens of tourist buses worth of visitors at any given time—customers mob the single ticket booth with two small windows, one unstaffed. The windows are low and small and cut in that half-moon shape that we associate with old banks that bad guys robbed in westerns. Around the window crowd dozens of people; those closest to the half-moon thrust an arm through, clutching the correct amount of money for the number of tickets desired, each arm risking being separated from its owner should the crowd shift suddenly to fill the space left by a customer who's begun to elbow his way out. The people in the crowd are like molecules of air rushing to take up the space held by that customer.

The only place in China I've regularly seen people in lines when they might be in a tightly packed crowd is in front of the ticket windows at railroad depots. I'd be lying if I said I knew why this place should be different from others. But there they stand, the ordinary citizens, in long lines, resting on or against the pounds of sacks and packages that Chinese seem to carry with them on even the shortest journey, the sacks reminding me always of grain, though they're really filled with clothing. Toting those sacks, the people seem to me as if they're running away from home.

I saw one such line outside the railroad station in Shijiazhuang, a town Smith and I were visiting. Following a young cadre from the Foreign Affairs Office of the college there, we cut into the head of the line, running low on time to find the train we were supposed to catch and obviously—by our looks—privileged here in the land of no privilege.

It turned out we were at the wrong gate, and turning around to walk back I saw them: in that long, snaking line with their bound bags and packs, all dressed in army green or dirty blue winter clothing, peasants on their way back to the countryside— the drabness, the gritty, weathered, tired faces in that line, and every eye, every one, hundreds perhaps, on us. Here was order, this line. It was a long walk back alongside it to the platform.

There's only one other place I've ever seen this kind of orderly line, even more orderly and neat than this one. That's the line in Tiananmen Square to visit the tomb, the visible body of Chairman Mao.

Elsewhere it's as though the limits, the borders of the body were collapsible, negotiable. The idea that each person, being an individual in his or her own right, should be allowed a certain small space around the perimeter of his or her body, space for breath, for inessential spontaneous movement, is, for whatever reason I as an outsider won't understand, not operative here.

Back from my travels, I'm in class on a Friday afternoon. I've just given a practice listening test to my junior students. A number of them have hung around after class to ask me to score their multiple choice answer sheets right away. In doing this, they're risking being out some money, since if they slip and speak Chinese to each other, easily done in the relaxed atmosphere after class, they have to put five *fen* into a box I carry with me marked "Junior Class Party."

I begin to mark one student's paper. "One is A. Two is D. Three is A," I'm saying out loud. Miss Jiang Xia, the sensitive student who some time ago confessed to me that "something was bothering her," is not scoring too high, as I don't expect any to on this, a pretest. The small crowd moves in closer at the sight of the paper covered with the black lines of my pen and Miss Jiang's mistakes.

I'm not up to number ten when I detect against the fleshy part of my upper arm the unmistakable feel of a woman's breast. I don't move or turn around. I slow my marking for a moment, almost stop, but then try to go on almost mechanically so I can concentrate on the pleasant tactile sensation—something I haven't felt for a long time, the closeness of a woman.

Later on, when I tell the story on bar stools or at the tap in someone's summer back yard, I won't add that it was through two sweaters and a winter jacket that I felt the sensation. The truth is that I hardly move, just make the sensation last as long as I can, then I think about it some more afterward—not about what it meant, but how it felt. Was it a come-on from pretty Miss Jiang? A lead up to sex for grades? Of course not. It was innocence, more than innocence.

The next day I'm going to the bank, walking a fast pace along the main highway through town, when I see a boy in split pants. Chinese children who aren't toilet trained wear such pants, conveniently split in the crotch, and it's not uncommon to see a little boy standing in front of his parent, watching himself send a high arc of pee out and into the dust. Nor is it uncommon at a busy place of commerce—a train station, even in front of a restaurant—to see a kid squatting down on the site. Somehow, this seems almost acceptable, a bodily function. You notice it for an instant, then turn away because . . . well, why dwell on it?

But this day I see on the way to the bank a boy who seems a little too old for the split pants he's wearing. He's bending over, playing with a stick in the dirt. His legs are straddled wide apart, and, as I pass behind several yards away, his bare bottom seems to be staring at me, mooning the world. I try to think about something else, and it's not until considerably later that I find what I saw that instant has stayed with me, like a photograph on a roll of film that stayed in the camera a long time before you developed it.

Pretty Miss Jiang's soft breast, through layers of winter clothing; a boy's bare ass, unblinking—these incidents betray a lack of self-consciousness in these individuals about the body. But they're contradicted by another tendency I see: that of my students to love being photographed, to be very conscious indeed of their images in pictures. It seems the only thing more delightful to many of my students than having a shot taken is to actually be given a copy of the picture. Smith complains that he shows Chinese friends his photos of them and then the subjects merely leave his apartment holding the likeness, as if there were no question about ownership, as if once seen, the photographs must certainly be identified as a gift. As if to say, "A photo *of* me is *for* me. If I take a photo of you, I'll give it to you!"

I've had amusing experiences similar to Smith's. Once I handed out a few pictures after class, group pictures taken at my Christmas party. I gave the snapshots to the subjects most prominently featured in each. But such a crowd formed around the desks of the recipients that the result was my being asked to have a print made for each face fully or partially visible in each of the group shots—sometimes groups of fifteen or twenty; I had prints made until the scratched negatives simply wore out. From that same party I had a candid snapshot of two students. As I was showing it to one of them, a group gathered tightly around me in the classroom. Suddenly an anonymous hand reached over the heads of the crowd and snatched the picture out of my hands. Then the owner of the long arm ran away. It turned out to be the second student in the picture, a woman of thirty-five, the mother of two, who confessed later, "I knew you only had one copy of the picture to give away, and I was afraid you'd give it to the other person in the picture, so . . ."

If you think about it, this interest in a picture of oneself is natural to anyone, and there are several ways to explain its pronounced presence among my Chinese friends. One is that photography is an expensive hobby here. What I see as a cultural preoccupation may be simply a matter of—forgive me Chairman Mao—supply and demand. People don't have many pictures of anything, so pictures are valuable.

Not only is photography expensive for the Chinese, but until fairly recently it was just plain unavailable. Brought up on Kodak do-you-remember ads in the States, we sometimes forget that life in most of the world has been just too tough for people to have access to a way to try to preserve it. I visited some friends, a young married couple, in their home—their one room apartment—and was shocked that their photo album contained only one picture of them together, a professionally taken wedding picture in front of a fake countryside backdrop. As an American, my natural reaction to the fact that people here don't have pictures of themselves is to think that not just the past or a memory of it but some part of them has been irretrievably lost. I don't want to repeat the past like Gatsby. But I want to take its artifacts, its baggage through life with me. As an American, I'm not sure I exist as an individual without tangible evidence that I existed in some past state of body, mind, and geography. I don't want to be so naked as to go forward without the assurance of those pictures.

In Beijing, in Tiananmen Square, in front of the Forbidden City, in front of Mao's tomb, and in fact in front of many places likely to draw Chinese visitors I find more evidence that Chinese people's interest in photographs of themselves differs from that of most Americans. In front of any such spot on a Sunday is a roped-off area large enough to permit pictures to be taken: me in front of the Palace Museum, me at the Monument to the People's Heroes, and so on.

The interesting thing is that enough space is allowed here in the land of little space so that a person can have his picture taken alone or with a friend or spouse—with no strangers in a position of prominence within the frame, no crowd. The poses struck by these proud subjects are seldom what we'd call natural—arms folded, back straight, serious look into the distance—a look suitable to the backdrop.

It's almost as though—in a land of exposed bottoms, a place where the immediate space around a woman's breast, or at least around six layers of clothing around a woman's breast, cannot be her own—in such a culture the photo needs to be not natural but better than natural. It's as though everything we in the West would call "body awareness" has been saved up in some personal reservoir, a postural hollow boot, to be drawn upon for this moment beginning approximately five seconds before the clicking of the shutter.

In the world after the photo and the world before, there is perhaps little place for a concept of oneself. It's culture, I suppose, but it's also that people here remain in many ways unsure of themselves, unsure not only of what the Party will allow them, but what they will allow each other and themselves. For so long those who might be a little better dressed, or even express evidence of a desire to be better dressed, fit for the sake of fitness, or happy for the sake of happiness—which must in any world include a happiness of the body—for so long any such person risked everything: criticism, denunciation, banishment. Even today my students tell me that those who habitually wear nice clothes risk the wrath of the Party Leader in our department.

But neither in this society do there appear to be those who will conceptualize about the body, who will make us worry about it, or worry that we're not worrying about it. The Chinese' self-consciousness about what they walk around in, like many of the material trappings of their society, is far less developed than Americans'. In this case I think their way is a better one. Their self-consciousness is to us the old-fashioned, out-of-date kind of our grandparents, or of the way in memory we insist on our grandparents having been—never falling into bed lustily, never in a passionate embrace of youth that they didn't know would fade or end.

The world of the photograph in China is another world. To the idealistic, maybe it's the China of the future; to the old, maybe it's the China that never was; to the gullible, maybe it's the real current China, the place of breasts and assholes being just somebody's misunderstanding; to the unthinking, it's just a photograph, and if you're going to have a photo taken of you, *this* is the way you pose. For a people who as a matter of policy are taught to disbelieve in the soul, maybe this is a world of the soul. The body in the real world, in contrast to that in the world of the photo, is for work and rest. Maybe for play. For procreation and for death. I don't know if death for the Chinese, for any of us, is work or if it is rest.

"THE PEOPLE NEED
AN ENORMOUS
LEADER"

One evening, two of my braver sophomores came by my apartment to practice their conversational English. They told me this night that they had once visited this same apartment the previous year to talk to "the American poet, Allen Jinsberger," and did I know him?

"Allen Ginsberg was here?" I asked. "Why didn't you tell me about this before?"

"Oh, he is a friend of yours?" one of the sophomores guessed.

Of course, I had never met him, but I found out later that indeed Hebei University had played host to poet and guru Allen Ginsberg for a period of time the previous winter. Ginsberg came on a State Department tour of China that included Beijing, Shanghai, . . . and Baoding. How he arranged such an unlikely itinerary I didn't know. This night, I tried to imagine these two sophomores knocking at this door the year before and asking Ginsberg the usual questions about how old he was, how much money he made, how many children he had, and so on, with little appreciation that the man they were talking to was one of the greatest of living American writers.

From this point on, I tried to collect as many Ginsberg stories as I could from my students: He practiced *qigong*, a kind of *gongfu*, with Yuan Zhenyi. He told some of the boy students that he hated

women. He gave lectures on William Blake and contemporary poetry, during which he chanted and shouted and beat on drums.
He was insatiably curious, asking questions on everything from
food to Buddhism. He looked younger than his age; he looked
older. He stayed for one week, two weeks, a month. He looked
strong; he looked weak. Though the impressions varied and were
even contradictory, they had in common that they were strong
impressions. Most were also highly favorable.

In honor of Ginsberg's visit the previous year, I added his name
to the reading list in the seniors' modern poetry class. I assigned
the students for our week on Ginsberg to try to read "Howl"—
whether they understood it or not—then, to write one page on
whatever they remembered about Ginsberg's visit. "Tell me," I
said, "about any personal contact you had with him." I wanted to
have a basis on which to judge which of the stories I'd heard to
that point could be believed.

"More tightly the students shrank into themselves," one senior
began her description of the winter night Ginsberg lectured to a
large group of students. "Before us stood the gray-bearded man
who looked a bit fat in no terms of obesity with his pot belly
dominated. He began to speak in his husky and wheezy voice.
Eyes focussed on him. He was simply dressed, but his bald head
seemed to contain great talent."

Ma Jingxian, one of my brightest and most perceptive students, described a similar scene: "Once he recited his 'Bomb,' I
clearly remember, he spoke so loudly that he was almost shouting.
'Bomb, bomb, who said bomb, we don't want bomb! . . . ,' a
poem protesting against war. He was so excited that his breath
got short and his face very red. I was excited too and showed respect to him: oh, that must be the high spirit of a poet."

She also told of the gossip and anticipation that preceded Ginsberg's visit.

The first thing I got to know of him was that he was homosexual,
which was soon spread all over campus, and I got a little bit afraid
of him because it was said that homosexuals were very eccentric. Several days later when I saw him for the first time, I felt he was the
same as any American. The only thing that I felt strange was that he
was wearing a long bright purple scarf. I don't know whether ordi-

nary Americans wear them or not, I just took it as his third sex characteristic.

Surely Lang Daying, my interpreter in the Foreign Affairs Office, must have been thinking of this same campus gossip when he accompanied Ginsberg to the railroad station: "As he left Baoding for another place, some amateur poets went to see him off. As they were to depart, he gave them warm kisses instead of shaking hands with them. The students were amazed and didn't know how to react. Everyone at present including me was impressed."

"Jinsberger" had shocked students in more ways than one. Wrote an older senior with an interest in the writer's method, "I remember clearly that in the lecture he said that if you wanted to write poetry, you must have rich imagination both rational and ridiculous. You even could imagine your penis (!) stretching out long enough to wind round all the lights in the room." And another student recalled, "He told us, 'Let's enjoy poems without thinking of parties or systems, for both Communists and capitalists will finally go to hell. . . .'"

Perhaps even more importantly, I found from my students' papers that I was not the only American who had been held under scrutiny at the weekly Saturday night dancing party. Ginsberg and I had at least one vital thing in common. One Older Senior woman wrote, "I was surprised to find that Ginsberg, this great poet and singer, was by no means a good dancer. He moved his potbelly and his unflexible legs unharmoniously. His clumsy action made all of us laughing. I could not help saying that he was the worst dancer of all foreigners there." But another student remembered it quite differently: "Once we invited Ginsberg to dance with us in our classroom. With the music of disco, he stepped his left foot once and kicked with his right leg once. His action was very simple, but harmonious with the music. He said, 'A dance, like a poem, is important in its rhythms, not in its forms.'"

These accounts made me envious of Ginsberg's ability to blend in so well, to become invisible—despite his eccentricities—in such a short time, seemingly to get along with a variety of people. As the student impressed with the poet's dancing ability put it, "Allen Ginsberg is the only person, including the Chinese, in the

Ninth Collegiate Webster's Dictionary that I spoke to face to face. It's an honor for me to think of this." One of my seniors who had already joined the Party and was impressed with the poet's politics seemed to understand his very complex feelings about that subject:

> I told him that we knew he was very courageous and was respected by a lot of young people. He said very modestly and humorously, 'No, I'm not courageous. I'm only a coward. If you say I'm courageous, I'm only courageous about being a coward.' He smiled, and looked kind, amiable and sincere. He made people feel at ease.

> Later, I learnt from a Chinese magazine that the government of the United States had felt anxious about Ginsberg's behavior and manner in China. They were afraid that Ginsberg would do something exceeding conventional rules and bounds, that he would chant in the streets. Actually, all he did in China turned out to be normal and even better than they had expected. Allen Ginsberg really left a good impression on our Chinese students. He brought the American friendship to China.

I hoped that I had done and could do as well as Ginsberg had at making people feel at ease and at making an impression on them—not to mention helping them to learn some English—even though I was, like him, a rotten dancer. But Ginsberg's visit was short, and the long-term resident faces other problems, maybe sees another side of student life in Baoding. The novelty of the foreigner's presence wears off. Students become much more interested in "free talk" about music and fashion than in books, papers, and exercises.

These problems with motivation stem in part from the overloaded schedule the students must follow. My sophomores, for example, have nine different classes totaling twenty-three hours a week. If this leaves little time for activities the Party may not approve of, it also leaves little time for independent study or reading. What's more, only one or two of the sophomores' classes are electives; most of a student's schedule is planned out for him or her for the entire four years of college.

So I try to forgive my students for their lack of ambition. I suspect that poor motivation is the rule here because there's little reason for students to excel; in fact, there are counter-incentives for them to do so, the greatest being that it's dangerous, that other students will think them to be kissing ass or showing off. Rumors can start, and rumors can effectively damage reputations. And students know that school performance doesn't greatly affect job placement or pay anyway. Many students feel their lives are closed off, know all too well the limited possibilities for them.

Many of my seniors who will not become teachers fear that after job assignment there will be little for them to do at their work units. They're afraid they'll have to spend much of their time reading magazines and smoking cigarettes, the way they've seen "tea cadres" do all their lives. So many workers on campus seem not to be required to *do* a job, but to be *at* a work unit. They put in their time, and they go home. Because I was raised differently, I behave differently, even in China. "I'm impressed with your attention to your *duty*," one of my students commented once. In Baoding, it seems, you're encouraged to do something not because it may bring you a measure of personal success, and thus of personal satisfaction, but because you "owe" the action to the people, or to society, which is really to say to the Party.

If a Western teacher can have a small measure of success lighting a fire under Chinese students, he will probably find it more difficult to light a fire under the Chinese bureaucracy, which exists on campus, as it does everywhere in the world, to serve itself. A prime example in my experience concerns the library and its handling of the hundreds of dollars worth of textbooks Smith and I each brought to use in our classes and then leave with the university. If we wanted to be reimbursed for the books we brought (in *remninbi*, we agreed—money good only inside of the country), we had to turn the books in to the library. But if we turned the books in to the library, we'd likely not be able to use them in our classes. Smith found this out when he turned his books over to the library in September and never saw them again. The reason: the librarians refused to touch the books because they were convinced the books were contaminated with AIDS. The workers would kick the boxes of books from room to room and into corners. Apparently Smith's shaved head had convinced them we were both infected.

But by far the biggest obstacle to success in my teaching in China was the obstacle of politics. Cleverly and completely some of the students could take any story, poem, or novel and make it fit the Party line they had heard at political meetings for a lifetime of Saturdays and more—no matter what I might say to try to suggest other interpretations. There was an amazing degree of conformity in the papers of these students. Even among those not inclined to see politics in everything, most were reluctant to take part in a discussion that asked that they express opinions (though this reluctance is maybe more a function of culture than it is of any political system).

My first encounter with strange political interpretations in student essays came in a batch of papers on a story by John Cheever called "The Fourth Alarm." The story is a monologue in which a man sullenly describes the experiences of watching his heretofore conservative suburban wife perform sexually explicit scenes nude in a seedy 1960s off-off-Broadway play. The ironic tone of Cheever's narrator is such that, although we don't sympathize wholly with the man, we obviously see the foolishness of the woman, who thinks she's creating great art.

Some of my students saw it a different way. What's more, those who chose to write on this story all saw it pretty much the same way—as this student did, for example:

> History has proved that when new things are born, they are always opposed mercilessly and even insanely by the force of habit. But the new things' victory can't be restricted. The new things always replace the old things. Advanced things always replace rotten things.

> Everyone can choose his work he likes. Everyone has his hobby. No matter what he does, he serves for people or for society. Bertha [the wife] plays a nude part, and serves the society to educate people and by spreading propaganda among the people. She was welcomed and praised and recognized by the society.

> His wife is standing as a great woman in the society. To develop new things and drive out the force of habit and old traditional way is a law of development.

To a Westerner this response is humorous in itself. But the problem for the teacher is that it appears identically in other papers by other students, papers about altogether different poems, stories, and novels.

One student Party member, for instance, finds the same conflict between the new and the old in Wallace Stevens' poem "Six Significant Landscapes." An old man in the poem, who to us might suggest wisdom and experience, to the Party thinker suggests recalcitrance and intractability. "We can see," this student concludes, "that the old man does not want to create something new. He only wants to enjoy himself in the shadow comfortably, seeing larkspur, blooming blue and white, which looks beautiful." For me, the challenge was to show how it might be a good thing for an old man to just sit comfortably and see beauty in the world. I found myself, a Westerner, in the ironic position of asking an Easterner if he thought the older generation should be respected for that.

In Ezra Pound's reluctant tribute to Walt Whitman, "A Pact," another student finds the same conflict between new and old, and finds Pound to be the conservative voice of the two. Walt Whitman, addressed in the poem, "is sure to be attacked because he represents a kind of new and progressive idea, and he is trying to get rid of the old social customs." According to this student, Pound realizes that "a new emerging force will soon replace him, and a bright future is coming. Walt Whitman is just that person who is going ahead. Now it's time for the people to march on." About "the whole society of America," the student concludes, "no matter what they are, they have united together. They have energies, capabilities, and power. They should exchange their ideas to head on together. The old ideas are replaced by the new ones."

Students found the same themes expressed in writers like Sherwood Anderson, Alice Walker, Flannery O'Connor, Faulkner, and Yeats. Although these responses were more the exception than the rule in student themes, it was difficult to know what to say about them. I'm afraid I responded poorly. How would Allen Ginsberg, or any other teacher, comment on the following interpretation of Robert Frost's poem, "Neither out Far Nor in Deep":

. . . The poet is like a very old man of much knowledge who is standing high on the top of the mountain above the seafoot, watching everything about. Beneath his foot, he finds the people puzzled, they want to find their goal, but just glare one way, know not what to think. The People need an enormous leader with a pair of keen eyes.

The people (by which Frost means Americans) don't believe their motherland at all, they want to get rid of her to go somewhere else. But by now they still don't know where they should go or what to believe.

Finally I concluded it was pointless to attack these interpretations and best to learn what I could and just somehow go on.

The book from which I was to teach my American culture class, *Survey of Britain and America*, was a combination of, on one hand, politicized generalizations like those I found in some student papers and, on the other hand, detailed statistics. After a long fact-filled chapter on geography, for instance, "Chapter Two—System of Government" began, "The United States of America is a bourgeois republic, where political power belongs to monopoly capitalists." The book presented no argument or support for the assertion because to openly disagree with it and with the other assertions in the book, as I did in my lectures, was unthinkable for my students. With a text like this to work from, I brought in as many outside readings and activities as I could. But since the students had to read the text anyway, I thought I'd better correct some of its misconceptions in my lectures. (Unfortunately the class was too large for discussion: forty students, plus some weeks an even greater number of visitors from all over campus, hoping to improve their English by listening in.)

After the opening paragraph or two of propaganda, the chapter on government went on to give a fair explanation of separation of powers, the bicameral legislature, and the like. The students had as much trouble understanding the Electoral College as Americans do, so we skimmed over it. Interesting to me, though, was the book's inclusion of the detail of how much money the president makes: "$200,000 a year, and he also gets an extra $50,000 for expenses and special use; but he must pay a federal income tax on the whole amount. He gets an added $100,000 tax free, for travel and entertaining, and is provided a home—the White House."

I doubt that many Americans know this much about the president's salary. But I suppose the editors included it to show that indeed America is run by rich men at the exclusion of the voice of any others. I think, too, the inclusion of the detail reflects the interest here in the material. One of the first questions a Chinese asks a stranger is "How much money do you earn?" Presumably, that curiosity extends to American presidents.

I wanted to illustrate the American two party system, given short shrift in the text, by holding our own class election with issues, primaries, speeches, nominations and elections. There was some quiet interest in the project, until we got to the point of actually voting for the student "candidates." I explained the secret ballot, passed around a hat, and then appointed a neutral group of class visitors to count the votes. There had been a lot of embarrassed grins throughout this part of the exercise, and finally a good third of the ballots were returned empty or held comments like, "I vote for neither candidate," "I don't care who wins," or "I don't believe in elections." This puzzled me until one student pointed out what our text had said about voter apathy in the United States. Later, he admitted that some students were reluctant to participate too enthusiastically in the exercise for fear that a jealous classmate would tell the Party Leader in the department.

The text told us that Iowa in the Midwest is the leading maize state, that buses have replaced streetcars for public transportation in many streets and towns. It defined "motel" and "outdoor theater," and told us which statesmen are pictured on which bills and coins. It described the phenomenal productivity of the American farmer, then added that in "buying and selling, he is exploited by big business." An excellent chapter on education was followed by one on the press that said that "*The New York Times* presents the viewpoint of the Department of State," that *Newsweek* and *Time* "have ties with the American government" and that the *Washington Post* "has a closer tie with the American Congress."

But by far the most interesting account of any presented in the text was that of American history. "The American Revolution," our text began, "was a bourgeois revolution, part of the vast struggle of the capitalist class in Europe to smash feudalism. The merchants and planters had always believed that a compromise with England was possible, but the people's demand for national independence had become irresistable," said the book. Later came the Committees of Correspondence, "a great demonstration of working class solidarity."

The book portrayed the Civil War as an economic conflict between "capitalists" and "planters." The planters' determination to "maintain their cruel system of slavery whatever the People's wishes were" led to a fight.

"For a time things looked gloomy indeed," reported our text. The South faced industrial disadvantages, plus it had "four million slaves who had to be watched and guarded." The North was "sabotaged by pro-slavery capitalists," but eventually "because of mass support, the Union Army began to win victories." The war "ended in the victory of capitalism," and it "solved the agrarian problem by means of bourgeois democracy." Unfortunately, though, President Lincoln was assassinated "by an actor called Booth, a tool of the Planters."

The Civil War, the book added, "is also known as the second American bourgeois revolution."

The book delighted in describing the emergence of trusts, the concentration of capital, and the imperialistic adventures of the U.S. in the latter part of the nineteenth century. No mention was made of the Westward movement, the rise of organized labor, or Teddy Roosevelt's trust busting days. The U.S. enacted the open door policy toward China in 1899, the text maintains, because it "actually wanted to take the place" of the other foreign powers "and have the whole China under its control."

We soon learned that the U.S. "did good business selling munitions to both sides" in World War I, which was the only thing that delayed its entry into the war. At war's end, Wilson's Fourteen Points were a scam to allow the U.S. "to set up its own spheres of influence" in the world.

When the Great Depression hit, "it began in no other country than the United States." In response, Roosevelt's New Deal was a program to "develop monopoly capital and strenghen its rule over the labouring people so as to prevent the U.S. capitalist system from declining."

The book then took us through the War and up to the present day: The Munich pact in 1939 was "a conspiracy unfavorable to a weak nation." The U.S. tried to remain neutral at the outset of World War II in order to "maintain its own strength so as to establish its hegemony over the whole world in the future." The war ended, though, when the Soviet Red Army "broke the German hold and entered Berlin in 1945. The Soviet Union declared war on Japan, and with the help of the Soviet Red Army led by Stalin, the Chinese people finally pushed the Japanese aggressors out of the land."

"The United States, too, had done a lot in promoting the formation of the anti-fascist front," the book conceded. "Nevertheless, the nature of the U.S. imperialism had made itself felt during the whole period of the War." The evidence for this is the tremendous economic boom that occurred in America because of its participation.

After the war,

> McCarthy, Senator, . . . and the reactionary forces in the U.S. intensified their persecuting of the communists and progressives. . . . But the reactionary force could not stop the progressives from struggling against them. Labour movement, students movement, black movement, etc. have taken place in large cities in many areas of the country since the war. In April, 1968 the assassination of Martin Luther King, a black priest, aroused a big black revolution against the reactionaries in the United States.

Meanwhile,

> After World War II, the U.S. took the place of the fascist Germany, Italy, and Japan on the world political arena and became a fierce gendarme in the world. . . . It carried out the policy of "cold war" and "containment" towards the Soviet Union. But before long the U.S. became weaker because of the defeats it suffered in China, Korea, and Indo China. The Soviet Union then posed a serious challenge to its hegemonic position.

I spent three weeks in class refuting this one-sided view of American History. I could see the minds of the students close up before me—either they were afraid to listen to me, or, more likely, they were bored with contentions on either side of political or economic issues. They no longer cared much for any political argument, no matter which version was the right one. Attendance dropped. Even the outsiders from other departments who had been sitting in to practice their English listening comprehension pretty much disappeared.

Finally somewhere in the twentieth century, in front of the entire class, I dropped the book in the garbage pail, bringing muffled laughter and even some quiet applause. I'd brought in my cassette player that day, and we began to talk about Duke Ellington.

When I was living in South Korea, a friend who had traveled and lived abroad wrote to me about cross-cultural experience. She said when she first went to a place, any place, she was astounded at how radically different things were from the States. Then, the longer she stayed, the more similarities she found. The only exception she noted was Canada. When an American first goes there, she feels right at home. Then, she noted, "Everything just gets weirder and weirder."

Few people can get beyond this step when living in another culture—the step of finding similarities and differences. Maybe some anthropologists can get beyond it; to a layman, it seems like a tough business. My conclusion is that it's impossible to escape our native culture entirely—especially, for some reason, for Americans—so perhaps none of us should make claims of objectivity. Experiences like my futile discussion of American history make me think it might be better to indulge our subjectivity and see things from the only perspective we can—in my case, an American one. I was born and raised in Wisconsin of parents of northern European stock. Can I really expect myself to understand how a Baoding-er looks at the world, a world that for him or her may not even reach the borders of Hebei Province?

THE ADVENTURE OF
THE SUITCASES

◻ I walk upstairs toward my apartment one late winter day, see Smith's door open, and hear voices. Inside are three or four workers from the Foreign Affairs Office, moving and dusting off furniture; the new Foreign Affairs director, Zhou, who is a big improvement over his revolution-era predecessor (the one who gave us frisbees instead of heaters last November); and Smith himself. Sitting in the entryway to his apartment are five old suitcases, some bulging, all covered with dust.

"Bill! You're not leaving?" I ask, half joking, also half worried. Smith seems to think for a minute,

"No," he says. Then he gestures toward the suitcases. "They apparently belong to somebody who taught here five years ago. When he left Baoding he just didn't bother to take them along."

I stare for a minute: there sit the suitcases. The scene reminds me of one from a French movie, a scene which has little to do with the plot, but which an *auteur* director just threw in—five suitcases, unowned and unaccounted for. Things like this happen to the foreigner in China: you're presented with a situation that doesn't seem to make any sense, and then asking about it you usually find the answer to be unsatisfying, to be one that creates more questions, as if Franz Kafka had written detective novels.

About five years ago, Zhou begins to explain, there was a guy who was teaching English in our department and living here in the foreigners' building with his wife. "Over the semester break they met a friend in Hong Kong. The man got offered a better job—as a lawyer or something like that," Zhou says. "So he just broke his contract, and he and his wife went back to the States. No one has heard from them since."

This sounds like a story with some of the details rearranged, and it is only a start at explaining the suitcases. Why are they in Smith's room? Smith himself looks befuddled by the invasion of his space by the weary luggage and the corps of cadres lounging around trying to look busy, but not trying very hard.

"We had to move the suitcases here to Smith's apartment to make room for the new Americans, Dennis and Longstreet, the young bankers," Zhou tells me. "They will stay in the fourth floor apartment where we used to store the suitcases and this extra furniture. So we will store the things in Smith's living room, which he doesn't use anyway. The bankers may be here very soon. . . ."

I heard about the impending arrival of these two only days ago and have managed up to this time to more or less put it out of my mind. I felt strangely defensive at the announcement of their coming, and that was the genesis of my nagging feeling lately that there has been something strange in the air. I should be delighted at the prospect of more company, of two more American faces to talk at. A few months ago in the dead of winter I surely would have reacted this way.

But now my reaction is different. I feel that since I've made it this far on my own, living with the isolation, I want to go the rest of the way alone. The fact that they are to stay for four months, these strangers, to be here after I leave, gives a permanence to their stay that means that they will come to have a stake in this place just as I have.

I find myself reacting in that American way I've come to hate, thinking, "I need my space." With only two of us here and with Smith being less outgoing than I, I get to be the center of attention most of the time, most anyplace I am. I am special here—a "foreign specialist," the literal translation of my title, *waiguo zhanjia*, has it.

And now—what if these guys are dashingly good looking? Wonderfully athletic? Charming and clever? What if they are better clowns than I am? What if all the girls develop crushes on them and it's terribly apparent? Certainly just their presence here is going to, for a while at least, take the spotlight off of me.

On the other hand, what if they're stupid and obnoxious? They are, after all, bankers. And they're young, and they have bachelor's degrees. What if they like Heavy Metal and talk about where they're going to be five years from now? What if they talk dirty about the Chinese women and act jocky and competitive toward the men? What if they turn out to be disgustingly American, changing their clothes every day, taking showers, cleaning their apartment? What if they voted for Reagan?

Just who are these guys? Who in his right mind would come to Baoding to teach economics as these guys are if he had a yuppie job with some big bank in New York, as these guys do? Do they think it's going to be—heaven forbid—exotic?

There's something strange in the air.

And what about daily life? Will the addition of two more big noses make it all the harder to get the necessary luxuries: a car to meet us at the train station, help mailing a package, my room vacuumed every other month?

Smith says maybe the hardest part will be watching the stages they go through and being reminded of just how stupid we were six months ago. I don't especially want to hear someone getting the tones wrong saying "*ni hao.*" I don't want to be at the *xiaomaibu* with one of them with everybody staring and him trying to buy his first bottle of beer, his first bag of laundry soap. I'm better than that now. I don't want the Chinese staring at me and thinking I'm like him, thinking I'm a . . . foreigner.

And there will be culture shock to watch them go through, particularly that first period before their senses have become annealed against the basic gray scum that is the landscape and environment here. I'll see the revulsion on their faces—at the mud streets, the broken windows, the spittle on the floor, the stench of the toilets—and have to be reminded I was like that, that half a year ago I hadn't learned not to see it.

Or worse, what if none of this is apparent, none of these reactions take place? What if they love everything and it's easy for them and everybody loves them, especially—a worst case scenario—the young women?

Or what if they're the most upsetting of all Americans to me now, confirmed Marxists?

The five suitcases sit, like weary travelers themselves. Motionless, they seem to age as I watch them, drooping and sagging. The dust on their surface seems to have grown from within them, or grown on them like moss. I notice one is torn badly along the side. They've been here for five years. They're probably no longer waiting for anyone. I can't help unzipping one of the bags out of curiosity: inside are clothes, wadded up as if packed in a terrible hurry by someone who didn't care.

Smith wonders why this junk has to be stored in his living room. I offer my huge, empty closets, but Zhou says he can't use them because in a few months, after I leave, my room will be used for other guests, and if he put the stuff in there they'd just have to move it again in four months.

Then Smith wonders why after five years the stuff can't just be thrown out. We both know better than to ask that question.

"Why, after five years, can't the stuff just be thrown out?" we ask almost simultaneously.

Zhou laughs. "That's a matter of foreign policy."

"We would need to get permission from Beijing, from a high official," he continues. "It's not that easy. There would be a lot of trouble, a lot of forms to fill out. And even then we may not get the permission. Better just to store the things. As you know, anything dealing with foreign goods . . ."

He's referring to the fact that imported foreign clothes, secondhand ones, were recently ordered by the Party to be burned all over the country. The reason given was that they were unclean and unhealthy. But the real reason for the action was probably fear of the AIDS virus, which the Chinese claim has been halted at their borders. Also that Western clothing, even used, is valuable here. The proliferation of used clothing could make some free market traders wealthy, while severely hurting the domestic textile industry.

So the clothes in their suitcases sit quietly. The stuff can't be destroyed without permission, can't be sent back without someone to send it to. It can only be stored. In a locked room, according to regulations.

That this doesn't make sense should surprise none of us. All the same, I'm sure there's something in the air lately, something strange that I breathe and my lungs send like oxygen into my blood and my brain, something we don't understand, like relativity, like gravity or magnetism once was to primitive people, like the zipper was when it was first displayed somewhere in Connecticut, mystifying the minds of the time. And I'm the primitive people, I'm the skeptical scientific community saying in effect that humankind can never get off the ground, calling for the return of the button fly.

There's a strangeness I sense in the nature of small events of the last few days. Not just the mysterious suitcases, the arriving bankers. Also two young women worried about gossip, also the content of a Pakistani movie, and a favorite student joining the Party.

Some of this strangeness is little more than amusing. Take Pakistani movies, for instance, which, like their Indian counterparts, are turned out at a rate many times that of Hollywood. I'm told that an average Pakistani crew—actors, directors, and the like—can make two complete films in a good week. The results are formulaic, banal, highly romantic: a young man, a young woman, disapproving parents, heart attacks, car accidents (this last occurring off camera where it's cheaper).

The strangest thing about the Pakistani movie we see is the conflict, which centers around a daughter and her widowed father who love each other so much that neither of them will marry. When the young woman does marry she misses her father so much she must run back to him. When she's dying after giving birth to a daugher, she hands the child to her father, confessing once again platitudinously in dubbed Chinese her love for him while the husband stands stupidly by like an orderly. The film flashes years forward to imply the now-aged father has the same type of relationship with his granddaughter, now a lovely young woman herself. In America, kinky. But in China, and apparently Pakistan, a touching tale.

Even before the movie we have strangeness more strange than the movie itself. The two women chosen to be interpreters that day for Smith and me tell us that they just came from a self-criticism meeting. Embarrassed, they hasten to add that they don't self-criticize very often. At their weekly Saturday afternoon political meetings—attendance required—they usually read reports from various Party conferences, or often they just read newspapers. But sometimes if there's nothing else to do, they have self-criticism. They take turns reciting before classmates whatever it is they've done wrong, or they make up things that they think will sound good, things that coincide with the theme the Party Secretary has brought before them that day: I haven't studied hard enough, I spend too much time reading books instead of studying the textbooks in class, I danced and ate lunch in the classroom, two years ago (like sin, there's apparently no statute of limitations), I didn't do a good enough job when I was chosen secretary of the freshman class so my classmates chose another.

Normally the sanctity of attendance at the weekly political meeting cannot be violated. But this day since our interpreters had to go to the Pakistani movie with the foreigners, they got to self-criticize first and leave early.

I'm not finished thinking about the story of the self-criticism, left as I am with a hundred questions, when the Pakistani film stops suddenly only about thirty minutes after it's started. On the screen, a sign appears in Chinese.

"Oh," says Li Fengyan, the student who last fall helped me cook my Chinese medicine and who today is my interpreter, excused early from self-criticism. "We have to wait for the rest of the film to arrive."

"What?"

"This film is very popular, and we have to wait for the next . . . what do you say, chapter . . . ?"

"Reel."

". . . the next reel to arrive."

I'm trying to comprehend.

"From Beijing?" I ask, still thinking about serious stuff like central authority, repression, self-criticism.

"No! From another cinema in Baoding. This film is very popular, and it's playing at several cinemas in the city today. We have to wait for the next reel to arrive from some other cinema."

And so it is I imagine those Pakistani actors up there, with nothing else to do while they're waiting for the next reel, doing self-criticism, waiting for their story to continue as if for some Bengali Woody Allen, the woman waiting to return to her father again, who's had a heart attack; him waiting for the second heart attack that he, like Bullwinkle the Moose, knows is "in the script."

And on my way out through the dark at the end of the show, I see a guy on a Honda 250 near the front gate, reel three in his front basket, twisting and honking his way through the departing crowd, headed for the Worker's Cinema across town, where another group of Sunday people sit in mid-conflict, de-fidgeting children and smoking cigarettes.

The cyclist is like an electron, buzzing and beeping off through the crowd there in his white helmet. What if the film canister pops out of the small front basket and rolls away? Think of the children, the smoke gathering at the Worker's Cinema. Could he use one of the suitcases in Smith's apartment to carry the film canisters, to make his job easier? Could he use the clothes in the suitcase, too? If he wanted just the clothes, we could stack some *Beijing Reviews* on the empty suitcases and use them as end tables. Things should have a purpose in the world.

That evening, after the afternoon of the Pakistani movie, I'm to show again slides of my recent travels in China to my students, and I'm also to show some slides of last year's New Year's Eve party and the Christmas party at my apartment. I'm off to the foreign language department to borrow an extension cord, and as I enter the building, Wang Mei, one of my dancing partners on Saturday nights, asks me aside.

I had showed to half the seniors, at my slide projection party the night before, a slide of her dancing. She tells me she heard the picture of her is very unflattering, and could I please leave that one out when I show the pictures to the other half of the senior class tonight? "Thank you," she adds, "I hope I haven't offended you."

Not at all. But it appears that without thinking I have offended her. It *is* an ungraceful shot, catching her in the middle of her head-jerking nervous laugh, that exaggerated movement that I like so much but which, robbed of its animation as one moment in a series of moments, makes her look horsey and awkward.

The picture is very dark—one of those for which you curse the flash on your camera for not working right (when it was likely your own alcohol-steadied hand on the aperture setting that brought on the darkness). I included the slide, unthinking, because it's the only one I have of her at those parties. I wonder at the gossip, the personal nature of the criticism she heard of that one instant of gracelessness. Later Smith, whose knowledge of Chinese is far superior to mine, tells me that the Chinese word for "criticism," *piping* is somewhat different from ours, that it has not necessarily the suggestion of analysis or clarification. He says the character is in part made up of the words for "slap" and "judge." When he tells me, I think of the students self-criticizing before their classmates and the Party Leader, and I think of my mistake with Miss Wang's photo.

That night I show the slides, minus the offending one, to the second half of the senior class. They are greeted enthusiastically and some students stay after the show, the number dwindling as we party past ten o'clock and on toward eleven. When finally Lang Daying, who is also the class "monitor" or leader, announces that those left should go, and those left get up obediently to go, one student, Xie Rong, produces from her back pocket a photo of herself she slipped early in the evening from a pile of snapshots I passed around the room.

Xie Rong is as bright and pretty as any of the other women students and one I've always suspected was more popular than, for instance, Wang Mei. I ask her why she hid the picture and didn't she think it was a nice picture of her.

"Yes," she says. "But I didn't want everyone *looking* at it all evening."

I don't know if that's because only she is pictured in it, arguably, then, alone with me in my apartment. But I laugh anyway because the gesture is so charming, just as she is. I have 'the urge, just as I've had many times, to hug her, which is of course out of the question. Although she is quiet and seems to me one of the many students—especially female—that culture and/or politics will not permit me to know very well, she appears to me always to be a coherent, original thinker not apt to merely repeat the line handed her by a superior, a common tendency here.

In fact, having some kind of amorous encounter with Xie Rong is something that Smith and I have joked about at meal time. The fact that this is not an option for either of us doesn't matter; the fact that she is intelligent and beautiful does.

A night or two later at the Saturday dancing party I learn from one boy in her class that among the names on the very short list of seniors whose applications for Party membership have been accepted is none other than Xie Rong. So here too, inside the dance hall the air has been tainted by that same bug of strangeness. I shouldn't be surprised by Xie Rong's actions, but I am. My best student, my sometimes-daydreamed-about, one of the handful about whom I imagine, as I fall asleep in my loneliness, that what I don't know about her is hidden only because it would be so unswervingly lovely to me. How can she listen and write and think in class the way she does, which is to say for herself, and be or even want to be a Party member?

"The country's getting better, but the Party's getting worse," the boy classmate says, the one who told me about Xie Rong's Party membership. But then he admits that he, too, has applied to join the Party. "Party members get better jobs," he explains. So how can I blame Xie Rong?

Just then Li Fengyan, my interpreter at the Pakistani movie, dances by. "Did you hear that she is a Christian? Is that true?" the boy classmate asks.

Actually I know that her grandfather was a clergyman, but Miss Li is also a favorite person of mine, so I say I don't know and excuse myself from the student and, for a time, from the Baoding rumor mill. Once again in so short a space of time I've become aware of the interplanetary nature of my mission here, of the dangers of galactic extraterrestrial loneliness. How many more of my students whose personalities are a blank slate to me harbor ambitions that I would dislike or not understand? It is, after all, their right. I see how dangerous a cultural or political time bomb of getting involved here could be: "Mom, meet my wife. She loves me. And she's a Party member!"

The day before, I'd seen the usual Friday movie, a videotape in English on two small TV screens in the department, shown in a small hot room usually crowded with eager young language students ready to be entertained and improve their English at the same time.

This week's film was to be *The Deer Hunter*, which I'd seen only once, years before. I'd looked forward to the showing and was surprised to see only a handful of students in the small room, so few that it was even a bit drafty.

The film began, and the first scene shown was the three friends trying to climb aboard the helicopter from a river in Vietnam. I was prepared for the long buildup I remembered to be most of the movie, but someone whispered to me that this was part two, the film being too long for one afternoon's showing here, part one having been shown some time late last semester. I realized, too, the reason for the sparse attendance; the print of the film was terrible, obviously a tape copied from a tape, a home pirating job by some foreign expert in a past year. The sound track was unbelievably distorted as well, and if I hadn't known the actors, I couldn't have recognized them here. If I hadn't seen the movie before and remembered the story, it would have made no sense to me now.

I considered the problems of my students with such a tape. Added to this was the fact that this is a film about inarticulate people, their grunts and groans against a backdrop of mobile homes and bowling alleys. It might provide my students pictures of American culture, but little in the way of practical language training.

Despite this, I was soon engrossed in the film. I hadn't been prepared for the sudden immersion into the world of Vietnam that starting in the middle of the picture brought, but this seemed to add rather than detract from the effect. It's said that the story of a good movie is told with pictures, and with the sound track so distorted, the pictures dark or indistinct, I began to think that perhaps a good film was made from something even more basic: shapes and movements.

The images unfolding this way seemed the perfect match of medium and audience: A foreigner in a far away place, I watched a film—barely distinguishable from random light and noise—about Americans in another misunderstood world, one with consequences far more serious for them than mine held for me. Around me were others, also misunderstanding, for any of a number of good reasons. I suddenly felt that seeing the film this way I understood it better. I felt glad the Chinese couldn't see and hear clearly because, involved now in a war with Vietnam of their own, they would misunderstand anyway. Someone might make of it merely something political. I felt suddenly that audiences in the States might also make of this film merely something political. Quietly, I went back to my apartment.

That's when I first saw the suitcases.

Now a saxophone player on the radio station from Beijing has just finished playing the "Theme from Love Story," his being what we used to call in music school, "vibrato you can walk through." He has a thin sound as if his reed were made of Tupperware. Between numbers is the polite Chinese applause I've grown use to—for this broadcast, as well or better orchestrated than the music itself.

I'm reminded somehow that in Kunming once I heard Western music coming from the dormitory of some young Chinese women working at a hotel. I was staying behind the hotel in the cheap foreigners' dormitory, near that of the young women workers. I was washing my face in the outdoor sink; one of the waitresses was brushing her teeth in the sink next to mine while from her window came the gravelly sound of Donald singing, "I'm a Macho, Macho Duck."

The saxophonist on my radio has given way to a singer, straining for the high notes on the bridge of "Rhinestone Cowboy" in English with a considerable Chinese accent: "getting card and letter from people I don't EVE-en know . . . ," and afterward comes again that restrained applause that this culture expects.

The suitcases are locked in my closet now, some of them. The workers came in during the day while I was out, and I don't know how many of them they put in there.

The owner is no doubt . . . well, where? Still in Hong Kong? I see him at a white-clothed table in an expensive hotel, five years with the same female escort from one of the local services. They're dressed well, and she never gets any older and doesn't promise to. He says, "Sweetheart, I'll never go back to Baoding."

Or, still with his wife, I see him in that partnership in the law firm back in the States. I see him trying civil liberties cases there, or maybe doing storefront work for refugees or immigrants like in a TV movie. Or maybe he's getting rich, as in life.

The lock on the closet—it's a small one, but it would have to be forcibly broken, and how would I explain that to Zhou? Still, I want to see what's been placed in my house as if I had asked it to be there, want to see as if I could control such events.

That night in a dream I'm standing there in front of the closet door when I hear a voice coming from inside. "Let me out," it says. "I haven't done anything."

I don't move.

"I haven't done anything. Let me out. I'm not the one who brought the bad copy of *The Deer Hunter*. It was here when I got here. And I'm not a Pakistani actor and I'm not a banker. I'm virtually asexual and my face was burned badly in an accident with chemicals. I can loan you money. . . ."

Six months in Baoding, why should I be surprised that, from behind a locked closet door, a person in a suitcase is talking to me? I turn away to leave, but now there is a second voice, too.

"Let us out! Who do you think you are, coming here like this? Do you think you can control what happens to you just by keeping that lock locked? Don't listen to all that silly gossip and political doublespeak. You don't have to. It's not your country. It's not your world. So open the goddamn door. I haven't done anything and neither have you."

JIANG XIA

◘ A few days later came the first dancing party of the new semester. The two bankers—likable guys, it turned out, who would, of course, have no ill effect on my life here—were not interested in going. I'd planned to go after a shower, a beer, and a few chapters of *As I Lay Dying*. But I got rather comfortable curled up in bed against the cold; it got to be nine o'clock, then nine thirty, then quarter to ten. I always have a hard time getting myself to take the two minute walk over to the dining hall. I feel so ridiculous knowing that *this is it*. This is my entire social life in China—no bars, no parties, no women that I'm allowed to fall in love with or even lust after, no going out on a date to a restaurant or a movie, no meeting new people since by this time I've met everyone in town who cares to practice his or her English.

But the strange thing is, once I get in the door of the dining hall, that is, the one door that's unlocked, with an iron railing leading up to it on either side, like a cattle chute filled with workers from town trying to get in without tickets (the girls have been warned not to dance with them, but it's no use because they're the best dancers); once I get past this incredible fire hazard—imagine a few hundred people rushing and pushing the way only Asians with generations of experience getting on crowded buses can do (I've seen children and old women trying to get off; *xia le*, *xia le*, they shout, virtually trampled by the crush of those getting on looking to take the odd vacant seat)—once past this, and past the embarrassment of searching through the grub of the crowd, that is, the young freshmen in their PLA shirts, fuzzy cheeked and somber, the dancers in down coats and winter jackets, who can see their breath as they tango; once past this, once reinitiated into the other-planetary reality that is my Saturday night here, my social life, life itself; once I've found some faces that I know, I begin to have a good time.

It's true there have been times I've gone to the dance, walked a quarter way around the perimeter of the dance floor, then shook my head in answer to the voice inside that doesn't like loneliness and gone back to my room for a couple of shots of brandy before I could return.

And once Guo Xiaoming said, upon seeing an older guy dressed in rags, obviously a worker or some kind of bum who got in who knows how, "That's terrible. It spoils the atmosphere." I looked around at the grease covered tables, the open February windows, the boys clutching each other tightly, and I had to try my hardest not to laugh.

Walking into the dance is usually a variation of those scenes for me, trying not to laugh, or trying not to leave in disbelief ("No, this is someone else's life," the voice says). But once someone asks me to dance things start to look a little better, provided she can lead. Put more accurately, I stop looking at those obvious things and concentrate on having a conversation—teasing my dance partner about her hair, her supposed boyfriends—and trying to put my feet down in the right places. The fact that I can do these dances at all never ceases to amaze me. "We have dancing parties every Saturday," Dean Liu had written me in the States, "at which you can enjoy yourself the whole evening." Strange to think I hadn't believed him.

This night it was short, round Wang Mei who led me through the fast four-step and the waltz. We must have looked quite the pair out there, twirling our fast circles—me getting dizzy and almost collapsing.

Wang Mei is amusing to me in many respects: her seeming immaturity, her adolescent silliness that's a nice change from the too-serious surface disposition of many of the seniors. Her unabashed comments: that I'm "naughty," that I'm a "typical American—very quick to anger and quick to forget about it again."

The fact that her observations, about me or about others, are so unswervingly accurate is also a point of interest.

Impish Wang Mei has crooked, ill-spaced teeth; a round, puffy face; and a round body that looks like a snowman's. Her appearance in itself is not special. But what is, is her refreshing lack of self-consciousness about her looks. In America this girl would be a wallflower—desperate and depressed, a hard luck survivor of adolescence.

But here she's a clown, a card; she states opinions clearly, and though not a deep thinker—she's not that serious—I get the feeling she's often willing to say out loud what's on everybody else's mind. Perhaps this is in part because her father is director of a foreign affairs office in another city, so that she needn't worry as the other students do about job assignments after graduation. Certainly she will work in his unit, so she needn't so greatly fear stepping out of line.

I think I have to give the culture credit, too, for her attitude about her appearance. Though the Chinese can seem very cruel in their descriptions of each other, saying about Wang Mei, for instance, "Oh, you mean the fat girl?" or about Lang Daying and his awkward dancing, "He's *very* clumsy, you know." Though they're hardly charitable in this respect, I think that they really don't consider these matters are a measure of a person's inner worth (in American culture we *pretend* these things aren't important, but everyone knows they really are). I don't think, for example, they'd make fun of Wang Mei if she had a funny-looking boyfriend, or make fun of the boyfriend's taste if he weren't as funny-looking as she is.

The Chinese I think don't care so much about such differences in people. They probably do stare at their handicapped. And they gossip terribly. But there are so many people around that just as the presence of beauty in some is more or less unremarkable, so the absence of beauty is not seen as a particularly serious deficiency.

Or if the Chinese do value the notion of beauty and lack of beauty as much as we Americans do, they certainly don't show it.

Or at the very least, no one remarks to my face about my awkward dancing . . . or why my favorite partner is funny Wang Mei.

On Saturday night in Baoding there is little concern for what we in the West would call public safety, so at the weekly dance you have that single unlocked door—and by this I mean one door, not one entrance—to and from a dining hall that may hold up to a thousand young people. Outside the door are the two metal railings, such as you might see leading up to turnstiles at a baseball stadium, and behind and running perpendicular to the railings is some hastily strung barbed wire, a minor attempt at keeping partiers from the locked and chained doors next to the one functional entrance. The entrance is patrolled by a couple of college student volunteers who themselves would rather be dancing. There are no professional security people, no police, no people in uniform of any kind. And this in a country many would call a police state, the country with the world's largest standing army, a country where not long ago soldiers helped peasants at harvest time.

There is no supervision or authority or crowd control whatsoever—for what each week past 9:30 becomes a crowd. I've shown up late again this week, and again a bunch of people probably without tickets have bottled up at the door, where the railings will let one or maybe two persons pass at a time. These rough-looking types (probably workers from town equally desperate for their one small entertainment each week) will not budge until they're let in. Consistent with the no-logic that is the logic of crowds, those with tickets are mobbed up behind, pushing and shoving, waiting and clustering. After a while most of them give up, and so we are left with small circles of disappointed students in the yard in front of the dining hall. They are all clean and nicely dressed, unable to get into their own dance, waiting for something to break within the crowd near the door, waiting for the roughnecks to either go home or overrun the few student monitors holding back their surge, waiting for luck to allow them in.

Occasionally the crowd staggers backward as the burdened guards try to move those in front away from the door. More gather and the crowd outside numbers easily a hundred. Then two hundred, all waiting. All this time, remember, those inside cannot get out—all doors except this one are locked and chained. And inside there are no toilets. Inside, in winter, open fires are lit in empty drums to take the chill out of the unheated, cavernous dining hall, the windows to which, consistent with the Chinese practices about fresh air or ventilation or something else I don't understand, are open. Smoking, of course, a national obsession among men, is permitted. Fire exits, it appears, are not.

Now the student monitors have closed the door against the crowd. The glass has been broken many times before and has been replaced by plywood. Those in front begin to kick at the locked door. No fists fly, but some open hands do. The crowd surges back again quickly, a few of its number forced into the barbed wire.

All along, some students and especially workers have been circling the building looking for an open window low enough and large enough to climb through. Now those in front of the crowd are being hoisted on one another's shoulders to climb through the transom above the locked entrance. They will straddle the transom, balance, then leap the ten or twelve feet to the floor, knowing that once inside the dance hall, they can't be thrown out because, as with China itself, there is no way out.

This is Saturday night on campus in Baoding. Inside, exciting this fervor from the crowd, is not a famous rock-and-roll group from the West, not free beer, not even a war hero from the Vietnam front, but a few colored lights in a filthy, drafty dining hall. I'm outside and I know all this. I know what's inside.

And I'm anxious to get in.

There are times in China when I want to pinch myself—no, times I want to shoot myself to see if I'm dreaming. There are times when others will use a sentence that presumes my location in China, and when this happens I feel a sudden chill as I realize that it's me they're talking about who lives here. For instance, someone who lives in Beijing might say to me, "Do you find that living in China you . . ." and I get that chill, as if that voice inside me were saying, I thought you were making all of this up, or,

Don't *live through* these things, just lie about them in bars when you get home.

There are also times in China I want to muster all my strength to jump as high as I can into the air to test the gravity on this planet. Times I want to do a double take like a character in a Warner Brothers cartoon.

Seeing the boys risk life and limb to get in through the transom, seeing the crowd mob and sway, the strains of "Skater's Waltz" drifting out from inside—this was one such moment. But fortunately by this time I'd found Jiang Xia, one of my junior students, the one who'd been so bold as to tell me once that "something was bothering her," the one who'd crowded close to me while I scored her practice test. I watched in silence for a while, then turned to her to make conversation, turning back over my shoulder occasionally to see if the craziness was still going on behind me, or if I'd just imagined it the first time.

I was teaching Miss Jiang conversational English this term, so it seemed doubly appropriate to talk. She looked pretty for the dance and I thought to say so, but then thought better of it. Finding myself studying her face, I asked instead, "Do you mind if I ask you a personal question?" And she said, "Of course I don't mind. I'm Chinese." And then playing conversational English teacher, I explained to her needlessly that in America we ask permission sometimes before launching off a personal question at someone. She said that in China they didn't do that.

"Do Chinese women wear make-up?" I asked. "I mean, are you wearing make-up tonight?"

The light wasn't very good.

"Yes, but only a little. We don't like women who have it all over."

"Neither do we . . . or neither do I," I corrected myself. She wore only eye make-up and lipstick. The pretty red cheeks were natural.

I told her that if I didn't ask questions like that I never learned about China. She didn't really mind at all, and to me the fact that I'd asked her meant something—that I was at ease, that for some reason I wasn't playing teacher anymore, wasn't playing foreigner.

She'd already told me how much everyone in her class enjoyed the class with me and that I was the best English teacher she'd ever had and a few other sweet things, and I suppose in thanking her I'd begun to break down some barrier within myself. She hadn't been my student long, so I didn't know her well. I'd noticed, of course, that she was bright and pretty.

By this time I knew we wouldn't get into the dance, and I was getting cold and she looked even colder, probably because her clothes were more stylish and thus less warm than mine. I suggested we go for a walk to warm up, then amended that soon to suggest we go to my apartment. After that it's difficult to explain what happened—though this is China, and between a man and a woman who aren't married not much is likely to happen. But something in me changed; things were happening without my thinking, and at some point I knew I wanted very much to touch and to hold her.

That's not permitted.

Despite that, and despite my vow to Dean Liu on my first day in Baoding, and before that to the people in the States who sent me here, my vow to "keep my hands off the girls," I'd made a decision almost without will, that I couldn't go on being surrounded by so much beauty without touching another person. My way of life to this point had been stupid and unnatural, I concluded—so much so that I'd begun lately to identify, as a teacher, with some of the characters in the works of literature we'd been reading in class. This makes for a dramatic presence in the classroom but is not finally, I think, a healthy sign. In Winesburg, Ohio, for instance, there's a woman who at twenty-nine, I think it is, finds that life has passed her by and, as Sherwood Anderson tells us, realizes "that some people are meant to live life alone, even in Winesburg."

Then there's Prufrock, whom I covered last week with my seniors. Living in Baoding, I've had more than one occasion to walk the "certain half deserted streets." And though the women are not talking of Michelangelo, they do come and go, and, speaking Chinese, they're mostly unintelligible to me. Most of all, daring to disturb the universe after six months as "the happy eunuch," as

Smith describes our station here, has become a larger and larger issue.

How should I begin?

I don't remember the stars that night on my short walk with Jiang Xia, nor did I think to notice. I didn't see if the moon had climbed higher or had gone to bed early like the peasants do six nights a week. I don't know what force it was that carried me along without my feeling a need to think or consider consequences (in China under the Party there are always consequences).

Miss Jiang is built in a way that, judging from her legs, especially the long thighs in her tight blue jeans, you might imagine her six feet tall. But she stands barely above my chin, and I am only five foot nine. She has a curious way of sticking her tongue out just beyond the teeth of her perfect smile—her so very lovely mouth—that, in short, is one of the most appealing gestures I've ever seen. It's appealing partly because she has little idea what she is doing, as all Chinese "girls"—they call them that more or less by cultural definition—must not.

I don't know what force carried us upstairs, no turning back, behind the locked door to the music, the dim lights, my offer of a beer (No, she'd drink *kai shui*, hot water). At last, sitting back on the couch, we fell into a long, warm, comfortable . . .

conversation.

I don't mean to say I was disappointed. I couldn't, by agreement with myself, think about it, so as not to think about the other agreement that isolation—or desolation— was forcing me to break: the agreement to be, finally, impersonal with everyone.

"I'm very independent," she said. And we continued to talk in this personal way. She confirmed much that I'd thought about China and Chinese women—much beyond just the wearing of make-up. For instance, that because she was here alone, she'd be more likely to talk. In a group, Chinese are reluctant to talk, expecially the girls. It's culture, for one thing. And also, it's politics: if you talk—if you say something beyond the push-button response that I get from all the other girls on any given subject, so much so that at times I feel their personalities indistinguishable each from the other—someone, if you talk, will no doubt be listening.

But we were talking alone, and the relative intimacy of that talk made me feel almost as if I were making love to her.

"Yes, most of my classmates have boyfriends and girlfriends," she assured me. "Yes, the Party is against it, but they can't do anything about it." We laughed. "It's the one thing the Party leaders can't do anything about."

(Actually, she didn't say "Party leaders," but just "leaders." That's the way people talk here, the understanding being that all leaders are Party leaders.)

"I'm twenty years old, your guess is right . . . and no, I don't have a boyfriend. The others who have boyfriends, maybe later they will have some tragedy happen to them. When they graduate . . ."

She didn't have to complete the thought. I understood that after graduation students could be assigned jobs anywhere in the province, maybe even anywhere in the whole country, without regard even to husbands and wives, much less boyfriends and girlfriends. What's more, the government, *The China Daily* told me, wanted to prevent such "unnatural phenomena" as "young love."

"But don't you ever feel lonely?" I asked.

"When I see them walking together comfortably I sometimes feel lonely, but then I just read books. I bury myself. I know that some tragedy may occur to them, and so I don't right now want . . . love."

Her using that word let me feel how our conversation had grown more personal than any I'd had here. I said that I would stay in China except for my loneliness here, and she asked me to talk about it, and I couldn't, and then we both laughed at my inability to express myself, almost as if I were another student of English and not, after all, the teacher. I told her how difficult it was to get a job teaching at a college in America and that's one reason I came to China, and maybe that's one reason I never married, because in our society it's hard; people don't all come to life with the same expectations, and if you move from job to job and don't stay in one place, maybe you won't be married.

"I have changed a lot since I started study here," she said. "When I came to college my dream was to be an interpreter, to go to the South after graduation to work. There, I've heard things are not so tightly controlled."

I said I was amazed at the strength of the Chinese people. Living under this system, they still seem to be happy.

"I don't think the Chinese people are happy. We are very sad. But there is nothing we can do about it. So we go on. I wanted to be an interpreter"—she stumbled over the word—"but I saw that was impossible. Now I will try to be a college teacher. The life is very easy!"

We both laughed again, and I agreed that the life of a teacher had its advantages.

"It's a good life for a woman in China. There is time to do the housework. A man in China does not want a woman who is too involved with the society. Teaching college is an appropriate job. It's very safe. That's what I mean when I say there will be no surprise for me or my classmates."

I asked her to explain, and she said that in getting their job assignments, the students wouldn't be surprised. "But couldn't something good happen, something you didn't think of? Or something bad?"

"There might be a surprise, but not a big surprise. We know what's going to happen. So we are very sad. But there's nothing we can do about it."

I thought of what Smith had said at lunch just that day, that maybe those who rebel in this system, the students who don't come to our classes, or who look at a newspaper while we're lecturing, who walk with their girlfriends at night and so can't keep their minds on their studies—maybe these are the ones to encourage. Those who, he said, "have some inkling that life is to be taken advantage of and not just waited out."

"Look at your hands," I said. "Are they chapped? Do you know what that means? I mean here, this red. 'Chapped' means to be made rough by the damp and cold in winter . . . no, they're not rough. . . ."

"It's just my skin," she said.

At that moment touch began, and my hands were covering hers and hers mine in all possible directions and ways. "I'm not supposed to be doing this," I told her. "I promised I wouldn't," and I told her about my vow.

"In your culture, such touching doesn't mean much, is that right?"

How to answer when the answer is yes and no? Our hands talked their talk, so smoothly, like folded gloves, and the irony was that, because she thought it meant nothing to me, it meant nothing to her, and thus in reality it meant much more to me than it did to her.

So she didn't back away, and I held her close in my arms. Was that OK? She didn't seem nervous or threatened as I thought she might.

"Maybe you are very excited," she said naïvely, "but I feel nothing. I only feel safety. I feel very safe."

I decided that was enough.

She was lying in my arms now. I told her to understand that she could come back anytime and we didn't have to do any of this and that was perfectly OK. I told her we'd have class together this week and it would have to be business as usual—stupidly using an idiom she couldn't identify. I said she could come by anytime, with a friend or, of course, alone. I didn't want to be a threat or a problem to her, but in explaining I sounded to myself very American and thus, here on this couch in China, very foolish. She said she'd come back sometime and bring some writing she'd done and would it be all right if I could correct it? I said I just didn't want to feel guilty and didn't want to feel like I was taking advantage of her, and she, misunderstanding, said,

"Yes, but you can control yourself."

We sat close and talked closely for what seemed like a long time. We talked about being lonely and about her dream, again, and then a little about my past, although again it was hard because I still didn't know where to start the story. In this respect it seemed strangely that my life had been too long already.

"Were you lonely in America?"

"Yes."

"Maybe when you go back to your country you can get a solid job and have a family. Then you wouldn't be lonely."

I couldn't explain to her why this wasn't true because I didn't understand why it wasn't true.

"We think the girls in our class are prettier than the girls in Class One. Do you think so?"

"There are a lot of pretty women here, but I hadn't thought of it that way. Maybe you're right." Then I told her that I'd noticed that she was one of the prettiest. She thanked me, and we held each other longer.

Earlier I'd wanted to kiss her, and she said, "I'm saving that for my lover someday . . . I think it's important."

In America, a man almost thirty-three can be embarrassed telling such a story without sex. Of intimacy without physical closeness, without sex. In eighth grade I went steady with Cheryl Johanski for two weeks. We exchanged rings, and my mother noticed at the breakfast table. Apparently her mother did, too. During the two weeks, I think we sat together once at a basketball game.

"OK," I said to Jiang Xia.

Later that night we'd go downstairs in time for her to go back home with the crowd from the dance we couldn't get into. We'd see Lang Daying, my interpreter and student, who with his idealistic Party purism would look askance at my bringing a woman from my room at quarter to twelve. He, twenty-two, who laughed once when I asked him about going on dates and said, "Maybe after graduation," he who'd been a faithful servant to me here, and I disliking him for his look of disapproval to her, and her having to make excuses, embarrassed even when nothing had happened, because he was a Party man and a student leader.

"It doesn't matter," I wanted to say to her, her head lying in my lap. "Save your kisses." And this even after the next day when I understood that she understood almost nothing that I had felt that night because, in that very way we Americans have, I hadn't understood it.

Save them for your lover someday. Not your husband, your lover. Did you mean to say husband? Did you mean the same thing? Save them for him, the lover, not the husband, and most of all, save them for yourself. If that's what you're allowed to save of yourself, when dreams are gone, when surprise is gone except for little surprises, when innocent touch is gone except for that met with disapproval, and because of that even the freedom to feel real loneliness is gone, the freedom to enjoy your loneliness and misery, and with that maybe the freedom to feel at all. If there's nothing you can do about it, then do nothing but save, and saving, savor it.

I think it's important.

"Mr. Terrill, I thought I couldn't go on the bicycle trip with you and the other students, do you remember?"

It was a few weeks later, and the student was a trusted friend of Jiang Xia.

"Jiang Xia said you got a letter from your boyfriend and so you'll be away on Sunday to see him. Good for you. We can go on a bike trip any time."

"But I won't be going on Sunday. I'll have to stay in Baoding, because the Dean won't give us permission to go home on Saturday night and return on Sunday."

"But Sunday is a free day. Nobody studies on Sunday anyway. Why won't they let you go? Did you ask permission?"

"If we ask they just say no."

"Is it Dean Liu who says this?"

"No it's . . ."

"The Party."

"Yes."

"What does the Party care if you see your boyfriend or not?"

"They say we should stay in the dormitories where we live."

"What do they tell you—I'm just curious—if you ask 'why, why can't we leave?'"

"They say we are students in Baoding and we should stay here."

"Why?"

"Only the students whose families live in Baoding can go home on Saturday night and return on Sunday."

"Why?"

"We can only go home over the long holidays. Like May Day."

"Why?"

"Because some students wouldn't go home even if they said they were going home. They'd go to other places."

"What's wrong with that?"

"They might go to Beijing or some other place."

"What's wrong with that?"

"Something might happen."

"What might happen? They might enjoy themselves? What's wrong with that?"

"The girls might meet some boys in Beijing or something."

"So?"

The student didn't answer.

"So what do they say?"

There was a longer silence.

". . . I think it's only a problem in our department, in the foreign languages department," she said.

"Why?"

"Because the students are very independent because they're exposed to so many ideas from the West and they meet a lot of foreigners. So the Party must be very strict with us. Our department leaders are the most . . . conservative in the University. They are . . . a couple of Marxist old men."

"But if our department is the only one like this, you should all go off some weekend at the same time, without asking permission."

"You mean like a student strike?"

"Something like that. When they ask you, 'Where are you going?' just tell them to go jump in the lake."

"What?"

"To go jump in the lake. In American English if we don't care what somebody else thinks of what we do, we tell him to go jump in the lake."

Neither of us spoke for a time.

"But if we did that, then when we graduated we would be assigned very poor jobs by the Party."

"I don't think they could give all thirty-nine juniors poor jobs."

"In Beijing there was a student strike."

"Oh, did you hear about that here?"

"Yes. It started as an anti-Japanese strike. Our Party leaders held a meeting after we heard about it; they told us if students took part in such a strike they'd be punished. The student leaders in Beijing were not allowed back in college."

"Well, I know you can't strike. I'm just joking. But someday somebody in this country is going to. Then maybe you can join them. Things can't go on this way forever."

"Why do you think so?"

Now I couldn't answer.

"There's nothing we can do. We are not big potatoes. We are just small potatoes."

"In English we say small potatoes and big *fish*."

"Or big *shot*?"

"Yes."

"*Dui.*"

I nodded.

"Sometimes it makes me very sad. For a long time I am not in high spirits. So I try not to think about it."

Both of us thought, and neither spoke.

". . . Well . . . since you can't go to see your boyfriend, you and Jiang Xia can come on the bicycle trip with us . . ."

"I'm sorry. We dare not. I'm afraid I and Jiang Xia can't spend any more time with you. Ever since we went downtown with you to the department store our classmates have been talking. If we go on the bicycle trip our classmates will tell the Party Leaders that we have been spending too much time with you. Then we will be criticized . . ."

I said nothing.

"If you were us what would you do?"

I said nothing.

THE GIRL
WITH WHITE HAIR

◻ In conversation class I assign my juniors to prepare for a "prophecy" game the next week. Each student in the class has written his or her name on a slip of paper. The slips are mixed in a hat, then each student draws the name of another student, as if for an office Christmas party.

Then the road takes a turn: each student must write a one paragraph prophecy of the situation fifteen years from now of the person whose name he or she has drawn; the student may discuss family, wealth, health, occupation, education, or anything else that he or she wishes. In class next week, each student will read his paragraph, and the others will have to guess the identity of the person written about.

The juniors seem to like the idea of the game, and when we are talking about it after class outside the classroom building, the interest is strong to the point that younger students stop by to listen, and the juniors explain the exercise to them in English (being allowed to speak only English within my earshot).

Then comes the inevitable fall. Several of the students say it will be quite easy to guess the identity of students from the descriptions—except for the part about occupations.

"That of course is decided by the Party."

I'm aware of this—from my conversations with Jiang Xia, with some of my older seniors, with virtually anyone else including Party members themselves. But I have been led to believe the students have some voice in choosing their future occupation, that their preference will be taken into consideration when job assignments are handed out.

"It's true we can write down a choice," one student says now, "but it will have little affection on what happens" ("*effect* on what happens," I correct him). "There is a committee that chooses . . . Dean Liu and the Party secretary and the teacher responsible for our class. . ."

"Well then it's two teachers and only one Party man. That can't be too bad," I say.

"We are afraid that Dean Liu has little to say. It's mostly the other two."

"Which teacher is it on the committee? One who teaches you intensive reading?" (the course that is most important in the English students' curriculum).

"No. One who works in the office," he says. In Chinese, even those who do clerical or manual labor are referred to as *laoshi*, teacher, if their work unit is an academic department.

"It's not one who teaches a class. It's one in charge of student life." By this he means one involved with political study. "And he's very young and wants to improve his standing in the Party, so he's very strict with the students and none of them like him."

I am sad because I know some of the best students aren't interested at all in politics and do poorly in those courses.

"The very political students have an advantage; they will get better jobs. Those who like nice clothes or popular music will be worse off. The Party leaders don't like them at all. And if two students are boyfriend and girlfriend—which is against the Party's wishes—then they will be aparted . . ."

"Aparted on purpose?" I ask.

"Maybe. The Leaders are what we call 'old generation.'"

Other students, some just by their silence, confirm that this is the case. A lull falls over our discussion, which has been cheery to this point, with humorous predictions about the future of different members of the class. I almost catch myself meeting the silence with the usual Chinese words of consolation, "Well, there's nothing we can do about it." I've come to despise those words, along with "We are just small fish," "We try not to think about it," and, worst of all, "We're used to it."

All at once there is nothing to say; for a minute each of us looks away from all the others standing there. I feel we're letting time pass so that the injustice, the obstacle in our conversation can be forgotten and we can walk away, each with the appearance of a smile.

The juniors laugh softly when I mumble to them that China needs another revolution. I don't phrase the idea quite that way, but hide it in a subordinate clause somewhere so it doesn't draw attention to itself. I don't add the logical completion of the thought, "a revolution to get rid of the Communist Party." I've never said those words here, and I can't get them out, almost as if I were Chinese and, saying them, would have as much to fear as they.

Later I sit on my porch overlooking the listless campus. "Death to the Party, Death to Chairman Mao," I write in a letter to Gwen. "Marx was a rabble rouser, a pamphleteer. Lenin was a cheap politico. Stalin was a butcher." I'm not trying to convince anyone of anything; it's just that I have to live here and I want to stay sane. That means I must be able to find in the world a consistency that is in some sense mathematical, in some sense moral. "Your Party has cheated you out of your lives, and will always cheat you," I imagine saying to my students and friends. "Power corrupts even beyond hope, the evidence of which is in your faces."

Soon students begin to volunteer to me more and more tales of their unhappiness with their lives and of the injustice of the Party on campus and in our department. Maybe word is getting around of my anti-Party conclusions and statements to individuals and even in class. The word may be out that I'm a good ear for those who want to unload their frustrations.

I'm in a badminton game with Miss Wang Mei, my loyal dancing partner, when a conversation begins, one similar to the one I had with the junior students after our prophecy exercise. Maybe these subjects come up because job assignments—which is to say politics and the Party—have been on the minds of the seniors day and night lately. As the juniors told me, the foreign language department's Party secretary—an old man who speaks not a word of any foreign language (some Party secretaries in college departments have no more than a high school education)—is in charge of job assignments for all thirty-four Younger Seniors. The consternation of the students is clear.

As we hit the badminton birdie between us, Wang Mei and I are expressing our sympathy for Miss Li Fengyan, my guide to the medical clinic last winter, my visitor to Walden East. Miss Li didn't pass her entrance exam to graduate school, thus she won't be allowed to take the test again for at least two years, and this means that like the rest of the students her future will be decided on the whim of the Party Leader. This means, too, that she won't be allowed to go home. Miss Li is from Henan Province, and our school is in neighboring Hebei Province. The Party reasons that if you go to school in Hebei province, you *owe* a debt to that Province (or "to the people" of that Province, they say) and thus should work for it . . . for perhaps the rest of your life. In the case of Li Fengyan, no one told her before she came here that she would likely not be allowed to return home.

The saddest part is that Li Fengyan has a boyfriend at home, assigned by the Party to work there. Baoding is a twenty-four hour trip by train from the city where he lives and works. There is no place within Hebei Province close enough to make a meeting between them more than just a twice-a-year occasion—Lunar New Year and summer vacation. This is their lot for the next two years at least. I asked Li Fengyan about the likelihood of her relationship with her boyfriend withstanding the separation. "You're young," I said. "Maybe you will find another." "Oh no," she replied. "We've known each other for years. And there is a good feeling between the families."

There's irony and cruelty to compound the sadness of Li Fengyan's story. It would be possible for a senior student to be assigned to Henan province, but only if the bureaucracy gives our department some positions in that province to assign to students. This in itself is unlikely. What's more, Wang Mei tells me, in wanting to go to Henan, Miss Li "has rivals." The Party has said that not everyone who wants to can be allowed to go home, and there are two other senior students who want to go home to Henan.

And they're both Party members.

So Li Fengyan hasn't a chance. She has the option of going home on her own, but she could only get part-time work, most likely translating, even though she wants to be a teacher and would make an excellent one. She would have no health insurance. And her refusal to submit to the will of the Party would be a black mark on her record always.

Li Fengyan even went as far as to get a letter from a school in her home town saying they would love to give her a job teaching there. The letter bore the chop of the principal of the school, a vital sign of "officiality" here. The job was not a particularly desirable one, nor a high paying one (almost no teaching job in China is), but it's all she wanted.

When she presented the letter to the Party Secretary, he laughed in her face, then criticized her for being selfish.

Li Fengyan is perhaps the most generous, good natured, and sincerely helpful person I've met here. She's incapable of doing harm to others. She's the kind of person you'd like to hug once every day, not to give her support—she doesn't need it, being extremely strong—but to reassure yourself that there is some force of good operating in the world. Besides being remarkably strong, Miss Li is also bright, hard working, and extremely mature for her age—about twenty-three I guess. She's among the favorite students of many teachers here, Chinese and American.

On the other hand is one of her two rivals who are Party members: he's lazy and irresponsible. Except that he's not lazy when it comes to manipulating people and events. He does only what he has to do, then depends on cleverness and guile to get him through, barely. As far as English ability and studiousness is concerned, there's no comparison between him and Li Fengyan. But when it comes to getting a job assignment as teacher or translator, if one exists for Henan Province, he'll win.

I'm learning a great deal during my badminton game with Wang Mei, us talking over the wind, slowly moving away from the others who are lifting weights and standing in circles hitting volleyballs during this after-class sports period. As the wind carries the birdie continually over my head and I hit it back to Wang Mei, short into the wind, we drift farther away from the others, farther away from the warm weather stench of the *cesuo*, the communal toilet for a number of families assigned to work and live at the university. Finally, after a while, we stop playing altogether and stand with rackets in our hands and talk openly, out of earshot of the others.

"There are a few in our class, those who were Party members or wanted to be, who all the time we were freshmen, sophomores, and juniors would run to the Party secretary whenever something good happened to them." Wang Mei says. "If they got a good mark on a paper, or won a prize or did well in sports, they made sure the Party Secretary knew about it. Even Lang Daying did it. A lot of the time. Everybody else hated these students."

I hate to hear this confirmation of what I've grown to suspect since the night he saw Jiang Xia with me, and even before—that Lang Daying, the young man who has been of such help to me, that his blind faith in the paternal benevolence of the Party is not only the force behind his selfless service to me and others, but also a requirement for him to gain power and responsibility for himself in Chinese society. A requirement that he's aware of.

"Mr. Sun Je (Li Fengyan's rival for a chance to go home to Henan) was the worst of all in our class," Wang Mei continues, "and he was the first to be accepted into the Communist Party. He always was running to the Party Secretary with good news of something. For three years he reported his own good fortune, as he saw it, and he told the Party Leader bad things about everyone else, personal things so that they'd be criticized every Saturday in the political meeting. If two friends had an argument, just something minor, not anything political, Mr. Sun would tell the Party Secretary, and the two friends would be criticized. They were told they should work together for the people and not be concerned about their own affairs. Mr. Sun told the Party Secretary any secret we might have. If a boy and girl became boyfriend and girlfriend, Mr. Sun told the Party Leader. If someone went off on Saturday night after classes and came back on Sunday night, Mr. Sun had better not find out, or the people would be criticized the next weekend for thinking only of themselves and not obeying their duty to be good students."

"Politics are important in China, for everything," Wang Mei says. "The students all hate the Saturday political meetings. But they dare not miss them. We have to study politics. And many students join the Party just to get a highter position in society. Advancement comes faster to Party members. To be a professor, to maybe get a chance to study overseas . . ."

"Have you applied to join the Party?"

"No, I haven't . . . not yet." She laughs guiltily.

"I know many students have, even those who think the Party is bad and getting worse. I can understand if you feel you have to."

"I just want to live a peaceful life; I want to live satisfactorily, but . . ."

The sentence remains unfinished.

Just as during my conversation with the juniors, I feel a cloud descend. So often lately: some new anecdote, some new evidence of injustice that is making the lives of people I like very much amount to far less than they should.

To ask what I can do is as pointless as the answer is certain: nothing. More and more my experience here is becoming like that of an otherwise happy man who is plagued by periods of hopelessness that begin without warning. Lately walking on campus, I seem randomly to run across people crying—to a friend maybe, to a classmate off in a corner or under a tree. I see people with long, impenetrable faces, empty stares—people whose expressions are usually brighter, people I know. Though these sights have surely been here all year, I'm seeing them only now because now I understand something of the despair that brings them about.

What I see is not American unhappiness, that born of loneliness or isolation. I see here a listless sadness, a sadness of having given up, a sadness that comes from outside the individual and that the individual can thus do nothing to alleviate. It's as though the mind has come to the illogical end of a logical process. There are only walls around it. And the walls can be seen through but not walked through. They can be touched and felt, but not described or talked about. There is no more rethinking or reconsideration to be done. There is only time that can pass so that the mind turns to its other functions—respiration, perception, imagination—and the mind learns of futility, and a time passes before it strolls down that same street again that leads to those same walls, that same blindness. That I am an American and am experiencing this frustration as an outsider no doubt makes me less able to accept it, makes me understand it all the less.

Today I imagine that the *yumaoqiu*, the badminton birdie, is the Party secretary, and I hit it back all the harder into the wind, so that even against a strong gust it's flying past Wang Mei's reach and falling behind her. What can I do? For myself, it's only a matter of months before I can return to other problems, the problems of travel, then the American problems of many in my generation—no job, no home, no clear direction in life. But for my friends here, these problems won't change. They won't go away.

I can hope that my being here, listening, showing my friends that there are other ways to think, will have helped. I can hope I'm helping the people who smile slyly in class when I make a remark with political implications, something that a Chinese teacher wouldn't be wise to say. Are they just snickering at my boldness? Or are they happy to hear that they're not alone in holding thoughts that are—dissident is too mild a word—illicit? If I say even tangentially that in American English we don't use the word "liberation" to describe the events in China in 1949, but that we say instead, "Communist takeover," those whom I know to be malcontents, those among my Older Seniors who already have jobs and don't give a rip for Party line, they, and not the Party inductees, smile.

Making friends here is like becoming attached to dozens of stray cats your landlord won't allow you to keep. When I get home, I know I'll cry for my Chinese friends as I watch through the years the inevitable conflicts and contradictions that will continue to besiege their country, the return to the left which I fear lies ahead, the maintenance of the instruments of repression.

A few days later I see a guy walking down the street carrying a bag full of rolls. The bag breaks and the rolls pour out onto the dirt. There is a moment of surprise, then the guy laughs. So do the others around him. It's not a cruel laugh. Maybe it's a laugh of sympathy. At any rate, the guy's laugh is a sincere one, not one that was meant to cover up some kind of unhappiness.

I've noticed that Chinese people often laugh at their own adversity, just as they laugh at the adversity of others. Someone trips and falls on the street. Hilarious. In a movie—probably a pulpy imported American movie—a guy is brutally shot in the chest. Absolutely side splitting. Zhou can't burn the clothes in the suitcases because it's a "matter of foreign policy," so he laughs.

I remember being asked once, as a judge at a speech contest, to stand up and extemporaneously say a few words about Lincoln's Gettysburg address. I say that thousands of men were killed in the three days of battle Lincoln was commemorating—some nervous chuckling ensues—and that in the American Civil War it was brother against brother. That line draws a big laugh from the audience. I turn to Smith in the front row, who sometimes can spot cultural gaffs before I can and ask, "What did I say?" He shrugs his shoulders.

There must be some cultural reason for these responses. I'm sure it's not insincerity or insensitivity. I'm also sure it's not, as we Westerners would like to think, that worldly things don't much bother the inscrutable Oriental. That's the same kind of thinking in our culture that allowed us to try to bomb Vietnam back into the stone age.

One night Yuan Zhenyi, a favorite student of Smith's and mine and one of the Older Seniors, comes by to tell us he has just been to Beijing and has found out why he hasn't been accepted to graduate school. It seems as though some students, actually many students, have "gone through the back door" (*zou houman* in Chinese) to get in. His test score on the supposedly highly competitive examination was higher than many of the fifty students who were allowed to go on to take the second qualifying examination. He went to Beijing to investigate because he'd heard nothing from the school after taking the test—no notice of passing or failing. Now the reason why he heard nothing was clear—because he had passed the test, but they needed to pretend he hadn't.

I'm having an impromptu party with some of the seniors younger than Yuan when he comes by and tells his story. He speaks quickly and forcefully and in Chinese, and he holds the close attention of his audience with the story of the injustice done to him. It's a story of anger told in a voice of Chinese anger.

Everyone, of course, laughs.

Not cruelly, but in sympathy with Yuan, who is also laughing. I don't think anyone is surprised at the injustice. It happens here as often as not, so there's no reason for anyone to be surprised.

"They invited me to try again next year," Yuan says, then everyone laughs again, even louder.

"Isn't there anyone you can appeal to," I say—sounding no doubt stupidly American—"anything you can do?"

"Nothing. It would be a waste of breath."

More laughter.

Li Fengyan is listening to the story, maybe thinking of the injustice to be done to her. She doesn't know whether or not to take the job assignment we both think is in line for her right here at the university. Her main concern is how to get back to her home, family, and boyfriend in the least number of years. Now, she says, the opinion of Dean Liu is that if she were to take a job assignment here, she should be willing to make a commitment to stay forever. She says her uncle was just last month finally allowed to return to his home in Henan Province after his tenure at Hebei in the "public English department," as they call the office responsible for teaching English to non-majors. His sentence away from home: twenty years. Miss Li fears a similar fate.

But, she concluded, since she had the opportunity to stay here and teach—a good job for her—she would, and she would try to get her boyfriend assigned here also. This would seem to be a great compromise. But for it she was harshly criticized by the

Party Leader, who said she was "looking for an excuse to stay at the university." So she told him she wouldn't stay here now even if she were asked. On her request form she asked to be sent to a big unit somewhere so that after a few years she could maybe "trade down" to a poorer unit closer to her home. In risking this, she will be at the mercy of the Leader of the unit where she is assigned. If he doesn't want to let her go, he can keep her there until one of them dies.

We also fear that the Party Leader in our department is angry and, flexing his near-absolute power, will send her to the worst of places, which in bleak Hebei Province can be quite bad. It will be up to Dean Liu to stand up for her and try to convince the two politicos that she deserves a better fate—that is, if *he* isn't angry at her for turning down the chance to work under him here at the university.

Still and again, I feel helpless. I almost wish I could laugh as the Chinese sometimes can. But because I am American, and even more important because I'm me, that's impossible. I talk to the walls, making speeches and threats to Dean Liu. "I know it's wrong and so do you," I rehearse my speech. "It has nothing to do with being American or being Chinese, nothing to do with politics or culture. It's just wrong and unjust and immoral. And I'm coming to you because you know better, because I think you're a decent man and have a sense of justice." But what can such a speech do, even if delivered in person rather than practiced in front of the silent wall?

That night Miss Li Fengyan comes by my apartment to drop off a paper. She looks tired, having been working all day on the paper and worrying about her situation. I feel tired too, feeling the summer evening heat in my apartment.

Smith is there too, and she asks us about our job plans for the next year and listens intelligently as we explain to her the problems and contradictions of being an outcast academic in American society.

"Do *any* Americans have a steady job?" she asks. Her misconception of "capitalist" society comes as a surprise. Perhaps it shouldn't; she's one of the least political people I know here and, like many Chinese, has little interest in political matters of either East or West.

Soon we are talking of her situation. Smith suggests that she write to the Central Committee, that this kind of intractable old-liner doing injustice to people is what they want to weed out of the system. I suggest that I will go to Dean Liu and try to reason on her behalf, or at least get some information about what her fate is likely to be. Embarrassed by the attention we pay to her which she feels she doesn't deserve, she laughs at both suggestions and asks us please not to trouble ourselves for her. I can see in her this evening the modesty that I love so much in this culture, and also the sincerity in her that impresses everyone, the genuine warmth and caring. I feel the trust she places in us, the almost-spontaneity that lets feeling flow into words and out of them. Some people—especially journalists it seems, and probably diplomats—write and talk about the impossibility of a foreigner getting close to Chinese people. They are absolutely wrong.

In a calmer mood the day after Li Fengyan's visit to my apartment, I go to visit Dean Liu at home and tell him of my worries for her. I don't tell her that I am going to see him, nor do I tell her that I went. I think I made the trip by this time more for myself than for her. Dean Liu assures me he will fight for her. We can hope for the best, he says.

Some days later I go to a film with some of my senior students; *Girl with White Hair*, a famous 1950 film that was later made by Qiang Jing (Madame Mao) into one of her model operas during the Cultural Revolution. Anyone in China over the age of twelve has seen the story in film or opera form at least four times—adults, many more.

Girl with White Hair is a clever story, quite well produced for the time, and certainly the rival of most American films of 1950. As film, it is obvious how and why it would make good opera: a simple story with sharp contrast of good and evil, an emotional story just right to allow a character to stop and give song in a plaintive or melancholy aria.

I have Li Fengyan translating for me, which is always a pleasure.

She interprets for me to the small degree that interpreting is necessary, so much the story tells itself—as I found with the impossible print of *The Deer Hunter* weeks before. In this story a young woman, the daughter of a peasant, is about to be married to the kind, strong son of a neighbor. The couple have known each other for years. There is a good feeling between the families.

But then the girl's father cannot meet his rent payment to the evil landlord. So the father is forced to sell his beautiful daughter as payment of his debt, the evil assistant of the evil landlord going as far as forcing the father's thumbprint onto the damning bill of sale.

The father kills himself rather than tell the daughter of his deeds; he can't bear to bring news counter to the levity of her wedding preparation. The girl, after finding the father dead, is dragged away to live with the evil landlord, who soon rapes her.

After botching an attempt to rescue the girl and escape with her, the boy escapes on his own and joins the Red Army, that fraternal gathering of souls. The girl's hair has turned white as she, herself escaping from the landlord's household, has hidden in a temple in the mountains, stealing in at night to take and eat the bread left by worshipers as offering for their ancestors. The simple people think the white-haired girl a ghost and fear her greatly. The landlord takes advantage of their fear to get them to settle their debts with him, saying that he can invoke the ghostly woman against them if they don't presently settle up.

The happy ending, of course, is brought by the Red Army and the boy, who liberate the village. The evil landlord is shown on his knees surrounded by the seething and vengeful villagers. The young couple, the woman's hair once again black, are shown smiling amidst a bountiful harvest in their work in the golden fields of the New China.

When I mention the irony to Smith later, I am not surprised that he was thinking during the movie the same thing I was. Surely Li Fengyan, seated next to me, didn't see it: how closely her situation paralleled that of the white-haired girl. The main difference between the tales is that this time there is no Red Army for the brave and noble boy to go off to join. As in most stories of war, the heroes are transformed after the end of the movie from being part of the solution to part of the problem. There can be no liberation, because the people have already been told they're liberated.

Neither do I think Li Fengyan's hair will turn white, nor will she become a ghost.

MEMORY

◘ A few days ago the painting crew whirled through my apartment, working for parts of four days on the doors and trim, one day each for the cottage green on the outside of door and window frames, and the pale yellow on the inside. They came in a horde and worked with a logic of their own invention. I heard not a word of English from any of them—not even hello. (My students told me yesterday that many people here, especially children, are not entirely sure what "hello" means; they just know it's English, so they say it—or sometimes yell it—as soon as they see a foreigner. It always seems to work.)

What's more telling about the painters is that I dare not try my Chinese with them, knowing they wouldn't understand my atonal dialect, which is akin, I suppose, to a non-English speaker pronouncing all words in our language with the same vowel sound. It takes a person of some instinct and intelligence to understand my minimal Chinese, I've found, and in saying that I don't mean myself a compliment. It takes a person, too, who has a strong desire to communicate, so difficult is the task to listen and decipher.

The painters are not such people, though now that they're gone I have a good feeling about them. There's something typical in that fact to me, something to do with the function of memory, or the lack of memory. It's that not only events are shaded by the passage of time, but even feelings. The very center of our lives, feelings are even more likely than events to be misremembered. Maybe as individuals we misremember our personal pasts and then suffer the same fate as a nation that forgets its history; we don't learn from it, we repeat its mistakes.

Today as I look from my back porch, the painters are working in the building across from mine. This building is an exact copy of the one that houses my apartment—as in fact most buildings in the New China seem copies of all the others. So when they paint the outside trim, it's almost as if I can look one week into the past when they were doing the same on our building. As I sit here mid-morning, the wind and thus the dust is down, the sky is clear, and the one large tree in the gray yard in front of the shack-like dorms of the part-time workers, just across the sidewalk, is fully bushed out in green, its top just below my eye level here on the third floor. This one tree is virtually the only thing green in sight in any direction.

Last night I stood at this spot where I'm now sitting and drank the last of a beer—out of the bottle, American style. A thin crescent moon shone in the western sky, and one bright star glowed off its tips, just outside the circle of where the full moon would be. Two of my favorite students, Li Fengyan and a friend, walked below; they didn't think to look up to see me, so I called to them. I remember this clearly.

The next day, today, the painters are working across the way. There is one man, the rest women, young women. They all wear baggy pants, green army suits speckled in yellow and green. All wear hats over their black hair. They each look like a vaudeville version of a tramp, like something comically exaggerated. Meanwhile, in the gray yard in front of the workers' slum, a little kid is squatting down to shit through his split pants, and crying out for his mother. He has shit exactly two adult steps in front of the door of the family's single room in the row of single rooms of the long slum building. He yells out and in a few minutes the mother appears. I wonder if she will spank him, but it's soon apparent he's done nothing wrong. She moves him over to a heap of rubbish—papers, cans, and the like: I can't see exactly what from this distance—where he continues to squat. A bird flies by. And a huge bumble bee, right in front of my vantage point. There's a good feeling about the event taking place with the mother and child, about the day.

The boy is finished, so the mother, a young-looking woman, takes out one of the short crude straw brooms they use in Asia (an implement I find almost impossible to describe in Western terms), and sweeps some of the ground-gray dust over the shit. When it's covered she sweeps it into the heap of rubbish, which surrounds three empty oil barrels that at one time were used to contain the rubbish. One branch of the full green tree has grown low and heavy to almost touch the rubbish pile.

Not a minute later the boy, who's dressed in bright red pants and a light orange top, is standing in the pile of trash, digging around with a stick, curious. Now the father has appeared—for these are part-time workers—and he lifts the boy from the waste pile and into his arms. The child begins to cry and the father points to the rubbish pile as if to demonstrate a point. Being American, I wonder that neither the mother nor the father has yet wiped the boy.

The father seems kind, even from this distance of fifty or a hundred yards, even as my father might have seemed close up. In a moment the child has stopped crying, and he reaches up from his father's arms to pull some of the very green leaves from the big tree in the yard. The one branch of the tree is pulled lower by the happy boy, but the rest of the tree does not move except for the constant small motion the wind makes in its more apparent branches. Everyone in the small Chinese family is laughing. A few moments later, the three of them are walking away up the concrete path that separates our building from theirs. The mother is dusting off the boy's bare butt with her hand, while the boy does his part by patting wildly the knees of his red pants, so that dust flies.

A friend told me that Chinese children grow up slower than ours, so that a child who looks one or two has the mind of a three year old . . . because he is a three year old. I think that's why they appear so precocious, so lively to us Westerners. But I also don't believe that what my friend said about Chinese children growing up slower is true. (Before I came to China, I had trouble believing, at the same time, contradictory facts.)

As the young father and mother bend down to the child, and the three of them dust him off before they walk, they speak to him in the short sentences and exaggerated inflection that is parental urging, giving instructions and perhaps stating in some simplified way the reasons for doing one thing and not doing another. Why, for instance, he should brush off his pants. All this I must assume without understanding the language they're speaking. But it's an easy task.

By this time the painters have moved to the next apartment, still in the building across the courtyard, but now the apartment diagonal to mine. I can hear them scraping and talking, young people's chatter. A week ago, in my apartment, they were a headache that followed me from room to room as they finished one window, then another, always near to where I wanted to work or sit. I couldn't get away from them because it was too cool to sit outside and read and because others' apartments were being painted as well. The weather was much cooler than today's pleasant sun, and I had to leave the windows open far into the evening so that the strong-smelling paint would dry. I had a slight head-cold—as it seems we always do here in China—aggravated by the cool draft and the lead smell of paint. I was tired and irritable, and the presence of the painters that day was another imposition.

Or it seemed so at the time. Today, farther away, on a sunny day, the painters seem workers fit for a Whitman catalogue. They seem almost—and this is rare in my observation here—busy. So the danger is that the earlier feeling will be misremembered. The Chinese would chide me at making so much that's serious out of such small detail. But the tendency to forget, I'm afraid, does not stop with the insignificant. My father had a bad memory all his life, and now as I get older I'm aware of becoming unaware of things that happened only a short time ago. Plots of movies and books, the order of events on a recent day, the order of stops on a recent trip, the source of some visual impression—all are becoming lost in the sea of thought and sensation that is my year in China. To say only that time has passed too quickly is cliché. But when I can't remember even what it felt like to first come here, that worries me more, especially as a writer. I find that on a good day, on a peaceful day like today, I can't recreate for myself the turbulent or depressed mood of a few days before—when, for instance, I wrote Gwen in my disgust at the Party and its unfairness to some of my students. Worse, on those unsettling days I can't seem to recall that there were days on which painters working and a little boy in front of his house seemed to lend a wholeness to the world. Just as it's important to know the lessons of history, I think to be secure within ourselves we must be aware always that there will be times that will be much worse than those we are in at any given moment. And there will also be times better. To do this we must remember what it was *like* to feel that way, we must recreate those moods for ourselves by recreating the detail from which those moods are drawn.

For a writer, to have a poor memory is a particular curse. He wonders if it's obsession with detail and the recording of it that erodes memory, or if it's the failure of memory that feeds the obsession to preserve experience. Whichever the case, the obsession is part of the natural—in American culture at least—desire to preserve the past. For an American, who virtually by definition wants to live forever, it's a way of fighting mortality.

In contrast, the Communists here, out of political necessity, have tried to do away with the desire to remember the past—with their didacticism about the new replacing the old, which I observed in my students' papers. They preach the uselessness of what we in America call nostalgia, reasoning that the new is always better than the old and the individual must continue the "struggle" against the old ways. Somehow for me, there's an irony in that this philosophy comes from a Party that has, in its revolutionary fervor, kept this society so backward, so *behind* the times and change. I know that even some Chinese, those who have found out about it, look at the progress of Taiwan and Hong Kong and South Korea, then look at the poverty and misery of their own country almost forty years into Mao's revolution and ask, "Why?"

Unlike the Chinese version, our American style of progress allows us to indulge our yen for the sentimental, the nostalgic. And so it is I'd like to be excused for preserving moments here, so as not to be misremembered, like the painters, or forgotten entirely, like the story of the squatting boy and his parents and the big tree. Just as memory works or fails to work from such details, I suspect our subjective impressions are drawn from them as well.

Soon it is night. Sitting on this same porch, I can observe evening activities—the last of the part-time workers at dinner in their yard, seated on stones. Food on metal plates steams from their laps. They remind me of cowboys, sitting there. Theirs are the lives in China that, unlike those of my students, I can know little or nothing about. They live in dim gray rooms I walk past on winter nights; they heave together to raise an antenna atop a bamboo pole; they are parents of toddlers in red pants.

I can also hear, now, the sound of one *erhu* from the building across the courtyard, the one where the painters were working. It's the kind of sound I'd like to pretend I hear often in China, but I've seldom heard it except at the opera. I wish I did hear it more often, so much more pleasing is it to me than the sound, in America, of a boom box going by outside my window in Chicago, disturbing my Bach or my ballgame on TV (I'm certain I could listen to my neighbor's *erhu* and watch a ballgame at the same time). Tonight there's a woman singing along with the *erhu*, the nasal thin pitch of Chinese song that all sounds alike to Westerners so that we marvel at them remembering that melody that is really all those different melodies.

At the same time I can hear a woman cooking on the first floor. But I can see only her hands and arms over the wok. Here too are lives I can never know. I wonder why she's cooking at this hour, and what. It's past 8:30, and I imagine I can smell the food cooking.

A dog is yapping in the distance. There's the usual sound of people clearing their throats and spitting as they pass three floors below on the walk between buildings. Spitting is a Chinese sound, like the language I don't understand, and which I thus don't hear anymore, like maybe the engineer no longer hears the engine.

Above, contributing silence, is one of the many bats that sail here through evening. Light, near transparent clouds are drifting past at a high speed that may mean change of weather, and that makes it look as if the moon is hurrying across the sky as the clouds pass in front of it. It's daylight savings time in China—the first time they've tried it. They decided upon it in Beijing one day and gave the country about three days' warning. It's applied throughout China's one national time zone, so that when it's nine o'clock in the capital, it's nine o'clock in the farthest reaches of western Tibet or Xinjiang. I realize at this moment that that must make, in summer there, a midnight sun, the only one in the world a function of politics instead of geography and the physics of light.

Here in Baoding, the change lends a summertime feel to mid-May, and seems to make all these activities possible at so late an hour, now nearly nine. In the winter at this hour some nights, I remember already being in bed with a brandy and a book.

THE LAST DANCE

◻ In China, as in life itself, there's no going to another bar. If you're not where the group is at a given moment, you must be at home. Or if you are somewhere else, all in the group know where. This means that you can't escape anything in China: your job, your town, yourself. There's little mobility in the average life, so there's little occasion to say good-bye, at least not in a permanent way.

You'd think someone who's had seven jobs in eight years—in three different countries, two of the jobs involving travel more than half the year—would already know how to say good-bye.

But I don't.

When I worked for the Commission for Good Books and Literature, I said good-bye thirty weeks a year, traveling coast to coast to train teachers in discussion methods for the classroom. Good Books was a non-profit foundation with an admirable mission: helping kids appreciate literature. The books that the Commission published were fine; even the class we "trainers" flew around the country to conduct was OK. But the job amounted finally to too many airports, too many Holiday Inns and Budget Rent-a-Cars— all strictly second class. Trainers burned out in a year or two, or if they didn't they were most often fired by a curmudgeonly group of administrators, whose uncharitable personnel policies brought

Good Books and Literature (GB&L) the nickname "Grab your Bag and Leave" from its employees.

At the "Grab Bag" our boss told a story about a guy who had to give up his job as a trainer because his wife couldn't stand to see him leaving every week. It seems that one day when she was a little girl, her father had announced he was leaving the family; it was a classic scene with Mom and the kids sitting around the TV set one evening, and the father coming out of the bedroom with a suitcase in each hand and saying, "Good-bye." The girl was marked emotionally by the experience, and years later her analyst cited this as the reason she couldn't stand seeing her husband walk out the door with that garment bag every Monday, headed for two classes in Rapid City or some such place. So the husband had to leave the Commission.

Traveling for Good Books—Monday–Tuesday in Portland, Maine, Wednesday–Thursday in Kilmarnock, Virginia; back home to Chicago every weekend. The next week, Gainesville and Columbus; the next Knoxville and Montpelier—traveling in this way was a pointless experience. I tried to write about it but found little interesting to say. I had my Walkman on the airplanes. I would use the hotel pools to try to lose some weight but then down two cocktails and a restaurant dinner every night. I'd wake up and know I was in a motel room, but couldn't remember where. I drank too much coffee but could still fall asleep on an airplane before it left the ground. I started, for the first time since childhood, eating candy bars. I read U.S.A. *Today*. The fifteen months left me with a wealth of bar stories—the kind that take place in bars, and especially the kind you tell in them—and little else. Except an instinct for survival. At thirty-one, I became streetwise in the air lanes. I was bored shitless.

So it was easy to leave to come to China, easy to leave Good Books, that is. I do remember my reluctance to leave the States themselves. I kept imagining that some unforeseen circumstance was going to pop up to delay my departure for a while, say about six months. I imagined political eruptions, airline strikes, being drafted to run for governor, or even being offered a tenured college teaching job. Mostly I imagined someone calling and saying,

"Take it easy for a while, the flight's been put off till next week."
I imagined someone calling every week to say that. I think I actually could have lived that way for a while, forever preparing for a
departure that was one week away, then one week away, then
one week away.

It's ironic to me now that I can clearly remember writing
to Gwen, "I wish I were coming back from this year in China instead of leaving to begin it." She had written me at the same time
and our letters crossed in the mail. "I envy you the experiences
you'll have in China," she wrote, "but I don't envy you having to
have them."

The irony I mentioned lies in the fact that, preparing for my
return to the States, I feel the same way as I did preparing for my
departure for China. I keep imagining that some clear cut reason
will make itself known for me to have to stay another year. I wait
for the phone call that says (and of course I have no phone in
China), "That trip home, that uncertain future without a job in
America—it was all a misunderstanding. We'll advance you fifty
thousand dollars and publish your next book on one condition:
put in another six months in Baoding."

I feel moony a lot of the time now, two weeks before my return to always-always land, my plane ticket in my dresser drawer.
I stare out the window, waste time playing (badly) the pump
organ in my apartment, grinding out "Here's That Rainy Day,"
"Over the Rainbow," "Don't Get Around Much Any More," and
anything else my ear can find in keys no tougher than D and F.

Despite a resumé that looks like a railroad timetable, I just
haven't learned how to leave, haven't learned to say good-bye. In
fact, the thought of leaving China and going back to the States
scares me.

It's like I've seen not a ghostly father, but myself walk out with
those suitcases in each hand. Seen it so often. And it's not walking
out on a family either, which would make it easier, because if you
leave a family for a year to live in China, or to go to a bunch of
Holiday Inns, which strikes me now as a lot sillier thing to do—if
you leave a family that means you usually have a family to go back
to. A reason to go back.

Instead, it's like I'm trying to walk out on myself—to go to another bar, which I've concluded is all but impossible.

Today, Sunday, I went to drop off some papers with Dean Liu— a few minutes' errand—and we ended up talking all morning. It's the first and only time we've done that all year, so it's likely a result of my uncertainty about leaving.

During our conversation—besides asking me to consider staying another year, which he always asks—Dean Liu said to me, "You know, if you had a steady job back in the States, I think you would have found that many of the girl students would have wanted to go home with you. As it is, they maybe felt they wouldn't be secure."

This from the man who had warned me to "try not to get involved with them, they get crushes very easily." I was stunned. But not so stunned that I didn't think to take out my pocket notebook immediately and ask jokingly if he could give me any names. I thought maybe I could show them my bank balance and my modest investment portfolio and maybe one of them would want to give it a shot. It's not much money, but stated in terms of *kuai*, it would sound like a fortune.

It was a strange thing to hear from him not only because it almost certainly wasn't true—was he flattering me?—but because I had come to the opposite conclusion, that despite everything, I remain on the periphery of things here, an ornament, a novelty, a small part of the lives of even my favorite people. I am, and this goes for Smith too, finally just an outsider. How different from the way I felt all year, especially at the beginning of the year, at the first dancing party when I met Guo Xiaoming, when all the students clustered so eagerly around me. I might have known from that moment that to be invisible here, to somehow blend in, is for the foreigner finally not possible. And it's the impossibility of blending in that keeps us trying and trying to do so.

I am told beforehand that this night's is to be the final dancing party of the year. I get there early to make sure I can get in, only to find that the doors are—finally—manned by uniformed police, and people are free to come and go as they please. The entire evening passes without disturbance. I find out later that the police are not really police, but students from the school for police dressed up in police uniforms. Nevertheless, it is now possible to dance and talk without having the feeling that the Cultural Revolution is taking place again outside, as I felt at last week's dance. Then, we listened to the rhythmic grunts of a tribe of young workers as they threw themselves in chorus against the locked and chained doors. Once or twice we heard the breaking glass of a transom as one of them pitched a stone. During my visit to Dean Liu I suggested that it would be a simple matter to station a few police outside the door, and if the "hooligans," as he called them, appeared, to have them tossed off campus.

"But we have no authority to do that," he said. "And if we do, then if we run into them downtown or something, they'll try to beat us up."

I wondered if that were true.

Once when I suggested to students that it would be safer to have police at the dance one of them said, "We have a communist country; we don't like to have police around all the time like you do in America."

This logic and analysis left me without words. It was only later that I thought that if you called the police here and said, "Workers from town are breaking windows and starting fights at our dance on campus," the police would likely say, "That's your problem," and hang up. Authority here, though omnipresent, is very territorial.

This night there are to be no problems at the dance. I come in and, instead of dancing, watch from the far side of the room, picking out the senior girls from our department, foreign languages. They have the reputation of being the best dancers at school. It's surely the Western influence, everyone thinks. As I watch them—always among the first on the floor—I feel vaguely paternal, as if I am somehow responsible for their having grown into such intelligent and charming young women. As I stand there, a couple of graduate students in the education department begin practicing their beginner's English on me, telling me things that I found out for myself last September. The flatness of their talk seems to work in counterpoint with the sophistication I see evidenced in the dancers:

"Why aren't you dancing?" they ask me, the same old first question.

"I'd rather just watch right now." (Who is Xie Rong's new dancing partner? She's probably bored, but she's not showing it.)

"What cities have you visited in China?"

(She looks fantastic in white. My clothes—hand washed twice a month—haven't been that clean since I got here. Many of these girls have one summer dress. At most two. Always clean and pressed. And they're living six to a room.)

"Xian is a famous city."

(That motion—how do they do it? Look at Guo Xiaoming whirl.)

"Before you leave China, you must visit Xian."

(There is Ma Jingxian with her new boyfriend. It looks so easy, so natural. But such a radical change in personality, from skeptic to true believer in love and life, so quick to fall in love. Maybe because graduation is coming up.)

"You are watching your students dance."

"Yes, I don't dance worth a damn. And why would they want to dance with me, anyway?"

"That's right. They want to dance with their boyfriends. It's the end of the year, and for the seniors, if they are not assigned to jobs in the same city as their boyfriends or girlfriends, they will be very lonely. They are in love, and we Chinese believe you only fall in love once."

Laughter.

(Laughter.)

There's something vaguely unpleasant, though innocently so, about people espousing beliefs that all but negate your own. If you only fall in love once, then I've been a fool many times. This much I knew before setting foot in China.

I excuse myself from the boys after their pronouncement and find Wang Mei, one of my usual dancing partners. She is a wonderful dancer, and I had thought before that, as lively and unselfconscious as she is, it didn't matter in this culture that she was not pretty. But this night I come to realize that it does matter; I notice that for the most part she dances with me—who's not beautiful, who's not a good dancer, and who's an outsider—or she dances with no one.

Our conversation turns to those others whom I have been watching, the more sought after ones who have been her class-mates and roommates of four years. Very easily I find my opinion of the evening—of the year of dancing parties—changing.

"Miss Fang was asked to be the girlfriend of that boy . . . there in the blue jacket, but she thought he looked funny," Wang Mei says. "Xie Rong has a boy coming to the dormitory to see her, but he is not so good a dancer, so she thinks she can get someone better."

"Does everyone make these decisions on boyfriends and girl-friends on the basis of looks?"

"No. Wealth and position matter, too. But looks are impor-tant. To everyone but me. I think true feelings are most impor-tant. I don't care about looks."

Something sad in me, something I don't like about myself, tells me that fate has forced her to this conclusion. I feel sympathy, respect. Also warmth. As we dance she begins to tell me some-thing about herself. There was one boy, she says, one year older. He was from her home city of Weichang. He had asked to be sent to another city after graduation because he thought he could "find somebody better" than her. But he'd been sent back to Weichang anyway by the authorities. Her father told her she should just for-get about him. There are times she is just so angry . . . , but then "I'm a sentimental girl," she says, "always taking the tragedy role in life."

We are waltzing, and that dance is easy enough that I can talk and more or less move my feet at the same time. So I tell her it seems to me if you care about someone, maybe sometimes it's hard to stay angry at them even after the person's done bad things to you. It just reaches a point after a while that it matters less to you. Maybe Americans think like this. Anyway, I say, I still believe that you can fall into this kind of love more than once.

Wang Mei doesn't answer. She is teaching me to tango now. No one else has been able to teach me before; I haven't let anyone try. By the time that complicated rite has passed, with its spins and turns once thought in the West to be daring and passionate, I have come to my realization that these dancing parties are, sadly, not what I thought they were.

In order to explain this realization I need to tell first about an American couple I met in Shanghai. They were living in Taiwan and traveling on the mainland. They were both Foreign Service people, and both struck me as negative and unpleasant. But we were talking about living abroad, and they said something that, cynical though it was, had a kernel of truth in it for me. I said I wanted to live in a country for more than one year because it took at least two years to find out what was really happening in a place. They said yes, that was right, and then by the third year you usually knew what was happening: nothing.

So it is that the process of discovery living in another place is like a comet moving in its elliptical path around the sun, passing by the planets of daily life and experience, landscape and language. The comet moves so very quickly, but the distances to cover are so great that it's a process measured in years. Much of the experience is vaporous, and the return voyage, the completed circle, seems to take lifetimes. The comet moves away from the sun, away from the center: cultural difference is *everything* in your perception, the difference it makes between peoples. And then there is the trip back: culture is nothing; people are the same everywhere.

Guo Xiaoming and Xie Rong, my senior student who joined the Party, are dancing with some seedy looking guys from town who know all the steps. They are dipping and twirling, each couple. The boy with Miss Guo is wearing a dirty sport coat over a T-shirt and faded jeans. He has a smart-ass look on his face, and I am sure I recognize him as one of the hooligans of last week, one of those who stood on another's shoulders to climb into the dance through the transom, or one who belted his slight weight against the barred playwood door from outside. But the boy can dance. He can almost lift Guo off her feet in the fast four-step, and she giggles and smiles; they're the first out on the dance floor, moving diagonally across—like a comet, burning—so that all can see.

He can dance, and she loves it. He is confident and young. The boy Xie Rong is dancing with looks much the same. Then they trade partners, and trade back. All for fun. Meanwhile Miss Wei Fengyun, Miss Guo's usual dance partner when the two girls dance together, is with a dull-looking older man. Easily explained: Wei Fengyun is, people in an American singles bar would say, dumpy looking.

What this dance is, is simply a meat market—little different in concept than in the States. There is a different idea of what meat is, to be sure. And the sense of barter must be far less obvious than ours—after all, it took me a year of Saturdays to figure out what was going on. Something I thought all year to be un-selfconscious and non-hierarchical, is exactly the opposite—it is terribly vertical. The order is clearly established. The girls get out there early in the evening with their good-dancer girlfriends. They strut their stuff, and the townies who know the steps break in and ace out the college guys, the townies trying to get their hands around the waist of a college girl—bright, pretty, and young. And if you're lucky enough, if you meet someone nice, after some time perhaps you make a "friend," Ni *de pengyou*. In this, though, the class distinction must hold, and college students only go with other college students. Like Ma Jingxian, one of my brightest Younger Seniors.

"What about her," I ask Wang Mei. "Does Ma Jingxian only care about looks? Hasn't she known her boyfriend for only a few months?"

"Not a few months. Maybe two. But she says she loves him very much. He's a Party member, and he gets good grades. He's a good dancer. She's very satisfied with the boy. She thinks he's very handsome."

Ma Jingxian had been such a mystery to me—extremely intelligent and articulate, yet reserved in a sad way so that until she wrote an "A+" paper on a Faulkner story in class at mid-semester, I hadn't even noticed she was there. After I got to know her a little better I found I never had a conversation with her that was not engaging, was not marked by her humility and warmth, her interest in everything another is interested in.

Then not long ago she came by my apartment alone. I'd invited her to come anytime, and come alone if she liked, so that she could talk frankly. "There's no hope," she said this day, laughing, half joking as she often did—she has the most developed sense of irony of any of my friends here—but the undercurrent of seriousness is unmistakable. "In China we have learned not to be hopeful," she said, "because then we'll always be disappointed." This sounded to me so much like what I'd heard from Jiang Xia last winter.

I made Ma Jingxian talk about herself, though she says always she's uncomfortable doing so, about why she's so quiet. "It's because of the Cultural Revolution. My father had written poems and some articles. So he was persecuted. I was bullied at school. Even after the worst of it was long over, I remained very much . . . in myself."

Ma Jingxian was not quite three years old when the Cultural Revolution started, and only thirteen when it ended, yet she feels it the most influential event in her life. I thought that the ill effects of those ten years were limited to my Older Seniors, those who had been Red Guards or who had been sent to the countryside for seven years to "answer the Party's call," or those who had been older when their parents were persecuted or separated. Or at least those who had their college years interrupted by it, or received a college education of slogans and posters because of it. I was surprised to hear how it could have changed one so much younger.

Here then before me was a bright and wonderfully cynical young woman in a land of politically manufactured optimism. A country where the sun is always shining tomorrow. I had little idea what she thought of me. But I wondered for a moment, if I could choose, if I were able to fall in love *their* way, which is to say once, forever, but over a period of time, of years, of getting to know the family, of getting to know the other so that it's not *falling* in love at all but more the descent step by careful step of a lovely staircase with its ending place in a river in which we're wonderfully cleansed and lost. I wondered if given that, she, with her fine sensibility, would have been the best choice of all, better even than Guo Xiaoming, than Jiang Xia. I remembered once that she almost beat me at Scrabble. I thought of Dean Liu saying, "If you'd had a job back in the States. . . ."

It seems that a single man as he gets older thinks that happiness between himself and a woman is something even simpler than he thought it was when he was young, a matter of a few common expectations about the world and each other: a healthy cynicism, some idea about the limits of things. "What? You're not married?" the Chinese say, and there's no way I can explain to them that though there is beauty in America too, people less often hold the common expectations that make a match. We want more than just a family and companionship, a reasonably happy, if uneventful, life. "Why don't you get married next year?" they ask as if it were a matter of my choice. How strange to me that they think I've chosen to live this life . . . and that I could choose to live otherwise. How American of me to think I haven't.

To marry a Chinese, though—that must be on the mind of every American who is single here. I can hear people in American society saying, "Oh, you just like that subservient kind of woman in Asia who waits on her man hand and foot." Nothing could be more of a misconception. Many Asian women I've met, surely the most interesting ones, like Xie Rong, like Wang Mei, like Ma Jingxian, like Guo Xiaoming, like Li Fengyan, have strengths of character that most of us in America—male or female—simply lack. To find a bright, strong woman and go with her to another culture and encourage her that here she can be anything she wants, that, ideally at least, being a woman needn't hold her back. To see her use the opportunities our culture provides while maintaining the virtues of her own—this is the essential excitement. This is what those who imagine Asian women as some kind of lifetime geishas don't understand.

But I won't take home a wife, and someday six months from now I'll think back to what Dean Liu told me and wonder if he had been right. I'll remember missed chances. And I'll also remember one evening with two of my Chinese language tutors, me asking a battery of questions about boyfriends and girlfriends in China, about lovers and marriage; they, graduate students, twenty-five or twenty-six, old enough to know answers. I found out later that each of them had already married their life-long boyfriends during the just-passed winter break, and despite our close friendship, they hadn't told me about it—the Chinese habit of secrecy, I suspect. They laughed through my questions about their "future" marriage plans.

The subject came around to college girls kissing their boyfriends. Did it happen? Maybe, but in secret, walking at night. I, dumbfounded as usual at the seeming asexuality of Hebei University, had asked if college girls were interested in kissing *anyone.*

"They don't want to kiss *you!*" came the reply, and then cascades of laughter.

I laughed too, though on many lonely nights I wouldn't have thought it that funny. I laughed the way the man laughs who spills a bag of rolls on the street. Could my tutors tell what I'd been thinking? Could everyone? Was it really that outrageous of a prospect? Smith said once, "I think the relationships we have with these young women are much more important to us than they are to them." One night soon before I was to leave Baoding, I found out he was all too correct. Ma Jingxian, Li Fengyan, Wang Mei, and a group of their classmates had come up to my apartment to watch a television program on the new color set the Foreign Affairs Office had just provided me. There were mostly girls in the group, and all English students except one. I greeted this student I didn't know in Chinese and English, and we shook hands. The others told me he was a friend of Miss Ma, her *pengyou.* Then some said he was a stranger. Whenever they said anything about him, they laughed about it so I naturally thought, used to being the center of attention here, that it was a joke on me.

"He's my friend. You look so surprised." Ma Jingxian said, smiling more broadly than I'd ever seen her smile, the pensive intense look gone from her eyes. "He's from near my home town."

I wondered what exactly she meant, but tried not to look like I was trying to think of something to say. It hadn't occurred to me that they were using the word "friend," *pengyou,* just as we sometimes do in English: to mean "boyfriend" or "girlfriend."

"Why is everybody laughing? I have the feeling you're playing a joke on me."

"No, we just like to laugh. It doesn't matter."

It's rare for me to be speechless, and suddenly I had the feeling that everyone in the room, which is to say everyone in China, saw my surprise at the sudden change in the character of Ma Jingxian, the suddenness of her finding a *pengyou*. I felt that everyone knew that I had been interested in this young woman, even though I hardly knew that myself.

"It's true," she said, holding up for me to see a gold bracelet which had "I love you" engraved in English.

The boy spoke no English as far as I could tell, and thus could only follow from our gestures what was transpiring. "He's from the law department," she said while the group stood by smiling brightly. "What do you think of him?"

"That's not a good question to ask!" Li Fengyan reprimanded, and everyone laughed, only the poor boyfriend left out of the joke.

Later Wang Mei, a skillful and knowledgeable gossip, would tell me that they had announced their love affair two weeks before after the Saturday dance. "Do you remember that one? That night the dance ended early because of the fight, and so the boy asked her to go for a walk, and that's when he probably said the words, and so they decided they're boyfriend and girlfriend. That night she came back to the dormitory very late, and so I knew what had happened. The next day he came by the dormitory—it was Sunday—and so everybody knew. Miss Ma is very happy. She's very satisfied with the boy."

Soon I began to find out from the better gossips among the students that even those I thought didn't have boyfriends, have: Xie Rong, an affair with a teacher in the philosophy department "for two or three years now." Another senior girl choosing between two different ones, one here and one away. Another having a secret one no one was supposed to know about yet but everyone did. Another. Another. The word was coming out because graduation was near at hand. Most hoped to be assigned to a job in the same city as their *pengyou*.

And yet their world, that of Ma Jingxian and the boy, seemed so obvious, so junior high: coming in late after the dance, wearing a bracelet that says "I love you" in a language foreign to them, stopping by the dormitory on a Sunday afternoon. Maybe she can get a job assignment in his town. "Miss Ma is very satisfied with the boy."

If they've been acquainted for only a couple of months, there's been no long secret "unofficial" relationship, which is one that both parties deny so that they have the option of breaking up without losing face, so that they don't have to face the gossips and the disapproving Party Leader. This then by Chinese standards, is rather sudden.

"Some go through the old, slow way, and others become attached suddenly," Wang Mei explained, "especially before graduation."

"Of course, it doesn't mean that they will marry," she added, "but probably they will marry."

Even Dean Liu, in assigning Ma Jingxian to stay in Baoding for a job, wanted to know that her new boyfriend would be here too. He had them already married in his mind. The parallel between the dancing parties and a single's bar in my own culture remained. Except that in America a relationship like this would end in a different way for young people. The rewards would be more immediate; the consequences less long lasting.

Among the many people I knew here, Ma Jingxian, skeptical and questioning, had seemed dissatisfied with the world in a way that I selfishly found the most satisfactory. I remembered her thoughtful essays. I thought of her small smile, her hesitation and insistence; her easy, finally-curable cynicism for everything. Except dancing. "When I dance," she said, "I can forget everything. Only dance is important. It's just that moment."

This Saturday night in Baoding, at the last dancing party of the year, I am surprised to find that I am jealous—jealous of the boy with Ma Jingxian, the one with Guo Xiaoming, with Xie Rong—because being American I naturally want all of them. Somehow these dancing couples represent to me a failure in my own life, one I don't understand yet, one I fear I never will understand completely. In life, as in China, there's no going to another bar: no one can escape past failure, as much as he might have come to China to put it aside.

And what about my dancing partner Wang Mei? She obviously told me her sad love story for a reason, said it was she to whom only true feelings mattered. Would I even in America consider her? Or am I too thinking I can "do better"? Am I "very satisfied with the girl's looks"? All year I've considered the allure of beauty, gotten to know these young women. It seems I've come to a meat market of the mind. Only I haven't brought a shopping cart.

A few days later Ma Jingxian drops off a paper at my apartment by merely slipping it under the door. I'm coming away from a tub of laundry, arms wet to the elbows, and see it there. When I open the door she is a flight and more of stairs away, with a classmate. They hadn't knocked, they say. I say hello in the way you say hello when someone is walking away. How different from the close talk of her earlier visit.

You can get a lot out of living in China, a lot of experience that someone else might envy you having, a lot that was tough to get. But I think you can't get love. You can't get love if you don't have it before you come. The problems you bring with you to China are the problems you will take away. They, like you, will be one year older. A guy told me that once in a bar in Hong Kong.

And in China you can't go to another bar. When Ma Jingxian and her new boyfriend leave the dance early that Saturday, we all know why, and can guess to where—out for a walk on the tree-lined road in front of campus that leads to the edge of town, out with the others who are walking and "talking love" as the young Chinese say. No one assumes, as Smith points out the next day, that they've gone to some other bar, as they might have in America. People don't have to mind their own business in China because no one really has any business, no one has much of anything at all. And with that I can see my comet heading out again, tail against the sun of common human experience—culture is everything. I didn't see them leave the dancing party, of course, but I found myself noticing that they were gone. I'm sure the Chinese did as well. I wonder how many of them, like me, were thinking—when he noticed, or when she did—not of the couple, but of themselves.

THE BACKWARD VIEW
OF LIFE

🔲 MY afternoon is unambitious—I tell myself it's the steamy heat: July in the sub-tropics, in Hong Kong. I wander around pretending to shop, trying to remember what it is I'm looking for. I buy some suntan lotion to convince myself I had something in mind. I walk into people, blame it on the hazy sunlight, then, hand shading my eyes as if in a salute, almost step into the path of a car, not reacting to their driving—unlike in the PRC—on the left side here, the car stopped and *I* almost hitting *it*. Even that doesn't bring me out of my daze. I stand outside a vegetarian restaurant, then walk around the block once before going in. I order the first thing on the menu.

After lunch, thirty minutes at a museum worth fifteen (the main exhibit hall is closed for repairs), and then a movie. It's Barishnikov as a Russian defector. I like it, and I like the cool and dark that take my mind away from me. I feel like a ghost shuffling around Hong Kong this way for a couple of days. My concerns are still in Baoding. I lie in my windowless hotel room . . .

At the left luggage counter at the airport on the way in to Hong Kong I met a Canadian journalist I know who's living in Beijing. We went out that first night for a bad dinner and some great beer at a British pub and talked, argued, and lied about China all evening—

six hours or more. I wondered when was the next time I'd have such a conversation, with someone else for whom China has become obsession. Halfway home to the States, I imagine that's what reverse culture shock will be: new concerns. Instead of finding the phrase to use to buy a shirt or take a bus, instead of wondering over one of the inconsistencies of Chinese politics, instead of trying to get young students to relax so they'll talk about themselves openly; instead of all that, I'll find myself talking to someone all night about fishing or Social Security or the new shopping mall. Or worse, I'll find myself talking for a long time about China to someone who can only ask questions and eventually yawn, not venture opinion or relay experience. No one can be more of a bore than a guy who talks endlessly about *his* China. Nothing can be more tiresome than me.

The Foreign Affairs Office tried to get a small bus to take me from my apartment to the train station because so many students wanted to see me off from Baoding for the last time a few days ago. Others would jump on a public bus ahead of time to be at the station before us. Still others would be on bikes, some maybe showing up at both send-offs, at my apartment door and at the train gate—or will it be the train car itself? I was afraid there would be as many as fifty people (good manners will not allow someone to get on a train unaccompanied, even if he's just going home for a long weekend), and I was afraid too that I would cry. Tears would have been thought inappropriate, so I prepared mentally for days not to cry, just as I had before my father's funeral. I thought about the Chinese bureaucracy; how I felt about the Party, the *China Daily*; the fatigue of trying to motivate students, of working against the system. I decided, in case all that failed, I would wear sunglasses.

My Chinese friends are not as sentimental as I am. And a further incentive for them not to be sentimental is the political one: nostalgia is sacrilege here. "The backward view of life," the concept my seniors found so difficult in Sherwood Anderson, is frowned upon. The religion of Communism says we can't look back; the past is the past and nothing can change it. "New thoughts and ideas replace the old," Lang Daying wrote for me in an un-likely essay on Robert Frost. "Thus the world is pushed forward. People are marching on. They look forward to their future."

I don't like this business of leaving, of marching on—it's too much like death. Yet every year or so I pack up and leave a place, feeling that if I can't go forward in my life ("modernize," they might say here) I at least must have change. It's the illusion of progress. I don't like this business of leaving friends I've just begun to make—dislike it so much that I may never go anywhere again, just for the dread of someday leaving. Or at least never stay long enough in one place so that the leaving matters.

Maybe because things change so quickly in America, because so little lasts long—marriages, jobs, apartments, championship base-ball teams, life itself since we live it so quickly and intensely—maybe because of this some of us Americans can become sen-timental about something that happened fifteen minutes ago. I know for me it's tied in with my poor memory, my blatant sub-jectivity, my feeling that I can't hold on to anything and thus must hold on to time so it can't move.

Li Fengyan and Wang Mei are there that next day at my apart-ment and then at the train station. Guo Xiaoming and other of my Chinese tutors are there. Ma Jingxian, without her new boy-friend. Yuan Zhenyi and a couple other of the Older Seniors. Smith. Lang Daying and our other interpreter. In all, thankfully, only about twelve—because I'm leaving during *xiuxi*, and many who would otherwise come are no doubt asleep. The cook waves me off from the front door. Jiang Xia and her friend, who were afraid of gossip from their classmates, did not come by, nor did I see Jiang Xia at the last dance. I doubt I will hear from her again.

On the way to the train station I see nothing. I take no last looks at things we pass, fearing even the brown-gray sights of dusty Baoding will make me sentimental. There is a false jocularity about the short ride—all talking about nothing so as not to be-tray emotion, then falling silent for long periods. Others ner-vously sing songs—"Auld Lang Syne" and "Red River Valley." One of my Chinese language tutors, a graduate student, asks me to pray for her, that she will be allowed by the Party official to re-turn home to her new husband now that she has her master's degree.

Everyone gets to go onto the platform with me. Then an old man wanders onto the tracks at the other end of the platform and seems to be unaware of the approach of the train. As it draws closer—it's the train for Beijing—Lang Daying, ever alert, ever the servant of the people, runs off to warn the old man, but taking my ticket with him so that we have to call him back when the train pulls to a stop.

I board the coach, then stand in the door for a long while. We talk over the shoulders of the two conductors in the door. I smile broadly not to cry. Smith makes some especially good jokes to lighten the mood. Lang Daying says, "Say hello to us for your mother," so I say, "Hello!" and we all laugh, and he corrects him-self, "Hello *from* us, *from* us."

I say that if the plane doesn't fly today or tomorrow I'll come back to Baoding. They joke that they'll have a welcoming banquet for me, show me to my apartment, and then say as people did that first day, "Would you like to meet your students?" Through all this, through the whole hour or so of my departure, Wang Mei says little, smiles little, but looks at me fixedly, as if seeing me for the first time. Then the bell rings, and I croak a good-bye and wave childishly.

"When you come back again, we want to meet your *family*," Guo Xiaoming says pointedly.

"Oh, so you mean I should find a wife?"

"That's right," says Li Fengyan. "Don't wait too long."

The night and following morning in Beijing I know will mean nothing to me after these moments, which, for some reason I don't understand, I know will always bring me a great sadness. The year has gone quickly. The year has gone. As the train pulls away, I put my arm out the window. Li Fengyan, who has said the least of them all on the trip to the station, clasps my hand as the train slowly moves away, and walks with the train for a few steps before letting go.

Which China is the real one? The one I complained about? Or

this one, the one that I remember now from Hong Kong, from outside, its warmth receding before me in memory. I complained more often than I felt involved, but I think now that I complained because I was involved. Someone who has made no commitment, who views China as a short-term experience which will end and lead him back home whether he's successful and comfortable there or not, for that person there's no need to complain. My letters to Gwen are filled with stories of injustice and loneliness because I lived most days as if the conditions they presented me were ones that would never get better or worse—in part the result of misremembered emotion, the lesson I learned from the painting crew. At the same time that these letters, this emotion, is shortsighted—foolish, the Chinese might say—it's also evidence of my involvement. At the same time I bitched about Communism destroying motivation, I worked harder teaching and living under Communism than I've ever worked in my life—worked for almost no money. It may have been something about my students that made me work so hard for them. Rather like the less they did, the more I felt I had to do to get them to do something. I think I did it as a way to avoid boredom, which is the reason we in the privileged West do so many things. And I think I did it for other reasons which I will never know or understand.

Dear Mr. Terrill

I am still teaching at the junior middle school where I taught before college days. I'd like to go to a school in which my English level can keep rising. When I asked for a transfer to the Teacher's College in the city, where the dean had arranged for my work, the authorities of my country thought it ridiculous. Later, through a grape vine, I learned that they thought me too conceited. Christ, is it fair! I feel packed in a room with iron window into a cage. In it I can only wish to see the forest and blue sky. If a tiger, I can bite with teeth and scratch with paws. . . .

Anyway, I am entirely absorbed in the literature you taught me and the books you left me. . . .

Yuan Zhenyi

There's a TV ad I remember from a few years ago, one for an American oversized sports car. Part of the ad shows a yuppie-type woman (so obviously a model) wearing oversized glasses and gnawing suggestively on the eraser end of a long pencil while eyeing a yuppie man stepping out of a Pontiac or whatever it was they were trying to sell. Sitting next to the woman is another man behind a newspaper. The woman jiggles around on her haunches, bouncing to some rock music that only she and we can hear—like someone who has to hurry to the toilet. The message of the ad is clear; she's with the guy behind the newspaper, but she's more interested in the other one with the hot car. The ad has stuck in my mind for years, maybe because it has all the basic elements of American popular culture rolled together: cars, ads, competition, sex. After a year in China I can see it more clearly even in my imagination, the message easily reduced to its lowest common denominator: let's do it.

Mostly since I've been back I've watched American life as if looking through the wrong end of a telescope. I feel as though it's all somehow temporary, that I can affect my own destiny in so small a way. Could it be that that very Eastern idea has crept into my very American consciousness? Or has the slower pace of Chinese life made me unfit, at least for now, for the American clip—all those cars, and all those people in them going somewhere by themselves . . .

Truthfully, it doesn't take long to become reenculturated. But in the process some interesting things can happen. The other day in Chicago I was about to set off on a series of errands when a friend announced that she had some things to drop off at the post office and was I going that way. "Yes," I said. "We can walk together," a very Chinese response, fully missing her implication that I could go to the post office *for* her, and she'd save time and be spared the trouble.

A few days later I was at the university where I used to teach, and after being the target of a good joke from a former colleague, one whom I'm not particularly close to, one who's a somewhat masculine, hunting-and-fishing sort, I clapped my arm around his shoulder as I would have done with Dean Liu or another colleague or male student in China. He backed away a half step impulsively before we continued our talk.

That night I was at a going away party for a married couple I'd never met before. During the course of the party, both the husband and wife were taking women, one at a time, into a bedroom and exchanging clothes with them—him coming out in a pastel jump suit, a sleeveless sun dress; she in a baggy T-shirt, and so on. Later a friend who knew them well told me the guy had sex with three different women in the course of that evening, none of them his wife. And so how *was* China, people asked me at the party, and I would stumble and babble in response.

Since I've come back to America, I've been walking around a lot in K-Marts and other department stores, trying to get a feel for the place again, totally fascinated at what is the best buy and how much the discount is—it's so mindless and reassuring to us Americans, so vitally important to the Chinese. Television seems nice to camp in front of, too. And I'm sleeping a lot.

One day in another city I met Gwen face to face for the first time since I've been home—in fact for the first time in years. I tell her that since China I look at the world, and at American women, at all women, differently. Some things that used to matter to me—being witty, being attractive—don't matter so much now. "*Mei guanxi*," I tell her. Other things that I'd never thought about much before now do matter. Like the ways that men and women are the same, and how it is that most people everywhere want the same things from life: to be comfortable, to have a chance to improve themselves, to see a better life for their children. These things matter. She says she's skeptical because I can't be more specific. She says something with me hasn't snapped back yet.

Dick,

Included is the rundown on job assignments for the seniors. The results weren't as bad as we'd feared. Almost no one got sent to the countryside. One of the two long-time "public" couples were sent to the same city, though it wasn't a desirable one—a punishment or not? The other couple were not sent to the same city, and the boy was back in Baoding to try to get his assignment changed. He was also suspected of having thrown a rock through Dean Liu's window. Basically, many students got to go back to their home towns, or the towns of their boyfriends or girlfriends. Li Fengyan got a good job . . . but not one in Henan.

Not much surprising about the bleak array of jobs—the big problem is the waste of motivation that comes from denying people the job they want to do. Ma Jingxian, among all those assigned to be teachers, got the plum job of remaining in our department—too bad because I hear she's not keen on teaching. Similarly, Xie Rong is set for life as a teacher at the school where she will do her graduate work in Beijing. She admits that she's very lucky to go to the capital, but her dream was to be an interpreter.

The other big problem is the impossibility of change. Who knows if this society will ever loosen up to the point where people can go from one job to another without facing a gauntlet of disapproving intransigent cadres.

And there were the expected injustices. Sun Je, the rat fink, got the best job, as an interpreter in the Beijing Water Department. . . .

Smith

My rooms have the flavor of abandonment: empty shelves, bare spots on the wall where I look to point out to a student some geography on a missing map, a new layer of dust from the neglect of packing, four days' worth of melon seeds and peanut skins on the carpet (this a Chinese characteristic). All but the dull Chinese propaganda magazines have been given away. There are spreading piles of papers around each waste basket, so that now whole corners of the room have been given over to them. There's the curious and random arrangement of chairs, where guests left them the night before: they look as if they're about to have something to say.

I've finished packing and assigning away that part of me which is assignable, as Emily Dickinson put it. I've given away to students and friends most of my books, cassette tapes, odds and ends like American pens and American coins. I've passed on to Smith my unused office supplies, a couple of trash novels, and an old suitcase, this last as much as a joke as anything.

I'd hoped for one last dancing party, where I could dance one time with as many of my students as I could fit into four hours—a kind of final examination of the heart, and for me of the calves, knees, and tendons. I wanted to try for fifty in an evening, and mostly, thinking of American pursuits on similar Saturday nights, I wanted to *count*. But unfortunately there was no last dancing party. Was it too hot? People too busy? There's never an explanation here for such a thing; it's just what the Leaders decide that day.

I've given out my address a million times, signed the seniors' autograph books, which are a wonderful touch reminiscent of our signing high school yearbooks. But here, the books are small and red, and the student carries his or her own pictures and trades with friends and classmates, who paste the black and white snapshot on a page of its own, the inscription from the pictured friend to lie beneath it.

"In a couple of days we'll knock at your door on the third floor," Wang Mei said offering me her book. "We'll hope to see your ghost. I'll yell out, 'Terrill, Terrill,'" and then sensing my sentimentality about leaving, she added, "I think you feel emotion very easily, you have the nature of a poet; we are intimates, so you must say a lot when you sign my book." I feel but don't tell her that I myself have become an open book in which people write, "Best wishes" and "Why are you leaving so suddenly?"

Dear Richard Terrill,

. . . as you know, in my city there are very few college students. Boys get married earlier than girls. They are after beautiful girls, not a bosom friend—a life partner. Though I really don't want to get married, it's very hard for a girl, even a boy, to be single in our country. If you want to be single many rumors will be upon you. If you have many opposite sex friends, you will be looked at as an immoral person. Oh Richard, I cannot help complaining about my fate. I'm in love with a boy, but I know he does not like me as I do. I don't know how to deal with this matter.

Perhaps you could send me some advice as what you did when you were my teacher. I think you are always my teacher. What a wonderful time we had in Baoding. We were able to talk about whatever we liked.

I think of you often. . . .

Wang Mei

"Would you please give me the parting words of encouragement?" Bai Zongbao so straightforwardly asked as he offered me his autograph book.

Bai was the Older Senior who each morning without fail spoke out first as I walked into the room, "Good morning, Professor Terrill," in clear English, loud as a radio, always with a never-forced smile, this right after he'd scrubbed the blackboard. Because he knew I encouraged people to speak in class, and because he knew that even in his very bright and able class few students would dare do so, he prepared each week a long question for me which he would proceed to answer himself, the answer no doubt memorized, trying always to encapsulate some main point about the story or poem we were discussing: "Frost is a poet of melancholy," his voice would boom from his front row seat, "therefore the beauty of the dark and deep forest is the beauty of death. Do you agree with my interpretation, Professor?" and then sometimes after I had spoken, "Thank you," he'd add.

I would always have to try hard to keep from laughing—at his elegant delivery, never at Bai or his ideas. Very short in a way that was a disarming contrast to his official-sounding voice and manner, Bai at thirty-eight was the eldest in the class. His father had been a Kuomintang officer, his elder brother, because of that fact, a suicide during the Cultural Revolution, and Bai himself sent to the countryside at eighteen. "I answered the Party's call," he puts it, using the phrase of that time, "and I was sent to Gansu Province to be reeducated," Gansu being in the remote West, poor and mountainous. "We suffered great hardships," he says, so clearly and strongly like a military man, "but we learned a great deal from the peasants . . . about practical things."

"We learned," he seems to announce, "how to survive." Eight years Bai was there in Gansu, first a cook, then a teacher, having taught himself English and been allowed as a model student and worker to go to college there for two years, finally allowed to go to a county near his home in Tangshan, but not to his home itself, so great were his family's crimes, so random the punishment for them. "Comrade Bai suffered a great deal during the Cultural Revolution," his classmates told me more than once.

The day after Dean Liu broke his arm in a fall from his bicycle,

Bai brought up the subject to me after his usual greeting before class. "Our Dean has broken his arm" he said. "We're moved."

. . . my daily life is going on very well. A couple of months ago I made a girlfriend who graduated from electronics department at my university. Smith saw her before he left China. But after several dates we separated. I don't know why. I've forgot her now, though she is nice-looking and well-educated. . . .

Lang Daying

I'm still single now. My previous boyfriend broke up with me because I can't go back to my hometown. OK. No problem for me. Now I'm make a new boyfriend. He is not Chinese, but he loves me so much I can't refuse him. Please keep secret for us. I know our marriage will meet with some troubles or cause a little bit sensation. I hope everything will go smoothly. . . .

Li Fengyan

I asked Bai Zongbao, and I've asked others of my students, if, when they return to their home towns, they ever see the people who brought so much misery to them and their families during the Cultural Revolution. "Yes," they always answer. "All the time."

"Don't you ever feel any bitterness toward them?"

Other students have told me, "The students in the Red Guard were just doing what the Leaders told them to do, so we think they are innocent. . . . It was just a crazy time. That's the only explanation."

But when I asked Bai Zongbao if he felt bitterness, he said, "These people have been punished." He spoke with his usual care and directness. "And so when we see them we can feel a measure of pride in ourselves."

I signed Bai's book, offering my congratulations on the accomplishment of his graduation and, I added, the accomplishment of his life. In return he presented to me as a gift something that he knew I had long sought after: two Cultural Revolution–era Mao buttons. One was heart shaped, to signify that "Chairman Mao is in our hearts," Bai told me. The other pictured Mao's profile over a small boat, showing that Mao was the great helmsman. On each button were the Chinese characters for "Loyalty to Chairman Mao." Most buttons such as these had been destroyed after the Gang of Four was overthrown. I held in my hands a cultural artifact, something that in twenty short years had become a museum piece.

"Don't you want to keep these?" I asked.

"No," he said. "We think they are silly."

"Aren't you afraid something like the Cultural Revolution will happen again?" I asked him later. It had, after all, been a time of unbelievable horror, affecting virtually every family in China—Dean Liu spending years as a cook in a lumber camp; our bright librarian only now finishing her B.A., at thirty-five, because during the Cultural Revolution she spent six years herding sheep in Inner Mongolia (the university gave her a job as reparation for the death of her father, a professor here harassed to an early grave by Red Guards); the lives of so many destroyed or disrupted as were the lives of my Older Seniors; as many as one million killed.

"It could never happen again," Bai said, echoing the Party line.

"But how do you know it can't happen again?"

"Well . . . we hope it will never happen again."

This same day, after I signed his book, Yuan Zhenyi presented me with his gift, a poem he had written several weeks before at the end of the term:

THE LAST CLASS

The last class
    had in the university

The last lecture
    given by American Professor, Terrill

The last time
    Bai Zongbao cleaned the blackboard for the teacher

The last poem
    taught in class is "Howl," written by Ginsberg

The last class, last lecture, last poem
last forever in our mind

What a different feeling I had held months before, the Saturday night in Baoding three weeks into my stay that I saw the Chinese movie *Song of the Revolution* with Yuan, Bai, and some Older Seniors. Having seen no other Chinese film at that time, I wrote to Gwen the next day, "I like the Chinese, and I wish they made better movies," wrongly thinking this one typical of their efforts. I told her I hoped for their sake that they didn't try to export it to America. "Even if a theater would play it," I wrote, "which it wouldn't, no one would pay to see it except for a laugh."

A film of the lavishly staged play produced in Beijing the previous year, *Song of the Revolution* was modern Chinese history done as a kind of stern and self-important Broadway musical, filled with singing and dancing. Like the play before it, the film was extremely popular, and there was not an empty seat in the Worker's Cinema on the night we attended. As the opening credits began, drawing applause from the packed Baoding house was no less than the "chop" of Deng Xiaoping himself on the screen, signaling his endorsement. This effort was indeed pure propaganda. Although well produced, the film's esthetic was stodgy at best. The choreography and dancing suggested a post-revolutionary Busby Berkeley: pretty comrades with great figures all in a circle and filmed from overhead waving red silk scarves back and forth in domino succession. The accompaniment was bad Western-style original orchestral music. There was in the film not a minute of the rich Chinese tradition of music, opera, or dance, which according to the Maoist line would have been considered old and thus holding back the glorious progress of the revolution. In short, for anyone who'd ever seen anything different, the film was remarkably tedious—all three and a half hours of it.

Song of the Revolution did have for me its moments: two stiffs in PLA uniforms—one man, one woman—frozen in make-up and reciting the narration stage right as though Shari Lewis had her hands up their coats—as though the producers were trying their hardest to prove the paranoid contentions of the radical right in America that everyone in China has been brainwashed. The obligatory minority dancers—Mongolian, Uygur, Korean—portrayed happily, of course, after liberation. And played, of course, entirely by Han Chinese actors. Also the crowd of prancing, dancing revolutionaries during the first Civil War, singing "Down with Imperialism" to the tune of "Frère Jacques." Something about the way the audience clapped along on one and three made me think at the time that it might be a long year.

"It's a popular tune here," Yuan Zhenyi explained, perhaps a bit embarrassed.

What disturbed me most was something about the figure of Chairman Mao, seen infrequently throughout the epic. Was it the way the audience applauded so vigorously every time he appeared that made me feel uncomfortable? I thought of my lovely student and Party member Xie Rong answering my protests at the failure and inhumanity of Mao by saying, "But without Chairman Mao, there would be no New China!" Questioning her assumption that this is a good thing would have been cruel at the time. And I thought, too, of one old professor retired from our department who, I was told, is still brought to the verge of tears at the mention of the name of the Great Helmsman.

What would Mao have thought of me sitting in the Worker's Cinema watching, capitalist and decadent and poisoning his revolution with my English, helping to skew the social experiment with my blue jeans and my whatever-I-can-get? Am I with my books, my cassette tapes and magazines, helping to balance the Russians on the northern border, am I Nixon's progeny? Am I important enough to incur his anger, making as I do ten times what my Chinese colleagues make, representing by my presence the wonder of money, of a better life achieved in some way other than his? Maybe it was just the actor who played Mao in the film, that he *looked* so much like a young Mao that I found disturbing: a broad face, the Larry Fine hair line, the stiff figure I so easily identify as Mao's—I'm sure from having seen so many still photographs of it, almost as if it didn't speak or move, but only posed, ever-straight like a personally threatening royalty. I'd have preferred a more animated sort in the role, an actor who'd bring some life to the part, remind me that it's only a movie, that my childhood fear of being overrun by armed men in laundry suits was rightly abandoned. There needn't be physical resemblance given the central nature of the role of Mao to the movie, of the man to history. Gordon McRae would have been nice.

I noticed that the guy who played Mao in the film was never allowed to sing or dance. He did smile, though, all the time, and was often surrounded by children, and looked fatherly. Maybe that's why the audience applauded at his each entrance. Even Zhou Enlai got to dance once, though he was made to do so awkwardly, I guess to show that Great Leaders didn't have time to dance, even though the PLA soldiers in the film danced through three wars—Western powers, the Japanese, the Kuomintang—and you'd think they were busy dying and didn't have much time for frivolity either.

Later, my juniors were studying American political campaigns in our culture class, a subject which, in their total hatred of anything political, Chinese or Western, bored them terribly. One boy asked me the good cultural question of, "What is the significance of American candidates kissing babies?" I said that it's just a way to get the voter's sympathy and approval—like the portrayal of Mao in *Song of the Revolution*: always holding little children, smiling and strong through the Long March, smiling benevolently as he walked among the peasants.

"Yes," said the student, one of the brightest in the class, "except that Mao really *did* care about the little children and common people. In America it's just politics."

To be fair, I couldn't tell him that he was wrong. I just wished that Mao had danced in the movie like everybody else had.

Several months have passed since you left China. I miss you very much. Your kindness, your lively class, and even your quick temper impressed me a lot. . . .

In a few months I'll be leaving Hebei University and be assigned a job, probably I'll be a teacher. I wish I could be a teacher as good as you are.

Here is a photo of mine which I forgot to give you before you left. Do you remember me—the sensitive and emotional girl?

Jiang Xia